AN ESSAY ON FRENCH VERSE

Jacques Barzun

AN ESSAY ON FRENCH VERSE

For Readers of English Poetry

A NEW DIRECTIONS BOOK

Portions of this essay were first published in *The American Scholar*, *The Kenyon Review*, and *Translation*.

Manufactured in the United States of America
New Directions books are printed on acid-free paper.
First published clothbound and as New Directions Paperbook 708 in 1990
Published simultaneously in Canada by Penguin Books Canada Limited

Library of Congress Cataloging in Publication Data

Barzun, Jacques, 1907–
    An essay on French verse : for readers of English poetry / Jacques Barzun.
      p.   cm.
    Includes bibliographical references.
    ISBN 0–8112–1157–6 (alk. paper). — ISBN 0–8112–1158–4 (pbk. : alk. paper)
    1. French language—Versification.   2. English language—
Versification.   3. French poetry—History and criticism.   4. English
poetry—History and criticism.   5. Literature, Comparative—French and English.   6. Literature, Comparative—English and French.   I. Title.
PC2511.B37   1991
841.009—dc20   90–48759
                                        CIP

87083893

New Directions Books are published for James Laughlin
by New Directions Publishing Corporation,
80 Eighth Avenue, New York 10011

To the Memory of
Five Adult Friends of My Childhood

Marie Laurencin
Georges Izambard
Albert Gleizes
Olivier Hourcade
Guillaume Apollinaire

CONTENTS

CONTENTS

. . . . there is in England a widespread
opinion that French poetry is merely
rhetoric in verse.
—John C. Bailey, *The Claims
of French Poetry* (1909)

Eliot wrote some of his early poems in French, and it is a common-
place that he and Ezra Pound initiated several generations of poets
writing in English to the moods and methods of French poetry—that
is, as the French began to write it after 1880. The result has been that
most readers of poetry in English know the work of the modern
French, a good deal of which has been translated. And the impression
is general that *good* French poetry begins with or after Baudelaire.

The appreciation of French poetry as a whole, even including the
modern, is thus marred by prejudice, misconceptions, and the
difficulties of the language itself. These last, as I shall hope to show,
are often unsuspected, which only deepens the confusion. In this
essay I want to marshall the facts and views that seem to me relevant
to this situation and try, with their aid, to clear the way to under-
standing and enjoying French poetry early and late.

That poetry in the French language existed and flourished for six
centuries before Modernism is not a new, revisionist thesis in need of
proof. Earlier critics never questioned the fact. The large-scale
influence of recent times upon English poets by the French was not
the first but the third occurrence of its kind. The first dates from
about the mid-fourteenth century, when Chaucer and his school took
fire from the great flowering of French poetry that had aroused all of
Europe in the preceding hundred years. In fact, Chaucer, Gower,
and others wrote in both languages, and their borrowings from the
French marked the permanent break of English poets with the forms,
rhythm, and tone of their Anglo-Saxon predecessors.

The second wave of influence took effect when the Stuart royalists,
exiled by the English Civil Wars, returned home, with Charles II as

the restored King. From 1660 on, he and his courtiers, besides importing French manners and speech, imposed on English literature the forms and outlook of Neo-classicism. Two minor poets in England—Waller and Denham—had indeed started earlier to write common-sense, end-stopped couplets, in reaction against the post-Elizabethan Mannerism. ° But the heroic verse dramas of Dryden and the satiric and ethical poetry of Pope and his successors were counterparts of French tragedy and of the "statement poetry" in use from Boileau to Voltaire. As for English Restoration comedy, its models were the plays of Molière and his descendants. In the lighter genres, the line is direct from La Fontaine to Matthew Prior and John Gay.

Currents from abroad did not cease to flow in the intervals between the three great floods. But influence in these secondary periods was less overwhelming. Thus the works of the French *Pléiade* in the sixteenth century found echoes in England, notably in Spenser; and as Harold Nicolson pointed out, "cribbings" from Du Bellay occur as late as the nineteenth century, in Macaulay. In that same century, Meredith and Swinburne show a good working knowledge of Victor Hugo. But by that time English poetry had broken with the French, and the dogma that none existed across the channel had taken root. Shakespeare idolatry and the new love of Germany had combined with the hatred of Revolution and Napoleon to persuade critics and readers that Neo-classicism and even what followed its demise were the antithesis of poetry.

Neo-classicism (so ran the argument) was a French invention designed to put a deceptive gloss on a native incapacity for lyricism. The two great poetries of the world were the ancient Greek and the English, with a few contributions from Rome and Germany. Forgotten was the eighteenth-century praise of the Italian epic and comic poets—Dante himself was little read—and Camoëns' *Lusiads*, like the Spanish Romanceros and quintillas, were left as curiosities for dry-as-dust historians. Dryden, Pope, and Johnson were non-poets too, and John Donne was but a name.

Such was the ambient in which the deafness to French verse was taken as a critical judgment. Since it still largely holds, on both sides of the ocean, for the first six hundred years of French poetry, the details of this earnest resistance deserve attention as pointers to what needs to be known or remembered.

°See Reference Notes, p. 137ff.

Begin with the self-assurance of this negative dogma. During a visit to the University of Cambridge in 1917, André Gide found himself seated at high table next to A.E. Housman. The poet and classical scholar, by way of small talk, asked Gide: "How is it that every nation has produced poetry except France?" Gide does not tell us what his answer was, only what he later thought it should have been.° For my part, I would simply have recited a good poem, for example, Du Bellay's sonnet, which begins:

> Heureux qui, comme Ulysse, a fait un beau voyage

and ends:

> Plus me plaist le séjour qu'ont basty mes ayeux
> . . . .
> Et plus que l'air marin la doulceur Angevine.*

Gide chose rather to match question for question and ask: "What is poetry?" Everybody would agree that the meaning of the term must somehow be settled if a perpetual begging of the question is to be avoided. It is not enough that English poets have again and again followed French leads; the hostile critics brush that fact aside and cavil on the basis of unstated or erroneous assumptions. Gide reasonably points out that poetry is not a constant but a variable. What mankind chooses to produce and call poetry changes with time and place and even with individual or group sensibility. On this last point, witness the anthologists, especially for what they leave out that others include.

The task, then, is to discern what poetry is, at least in the Western tradition. The problem, regrettably, has always been met head-on, by giving definitions, and these have proved unsatisfactory. Perhaps a bit of indirection might succeed better. For as everybody also agrees, whereas translating prose is certainly possible, translating poetry is not. What makes this true? What does the poetic original contain that is out of reach?

Happy the man who like Ulysses has traveled far. . . . / Much more to me is the spot where my ancestors built. . . . / And more than the sea breezes the soft air of Anjou.

*I shall give as footnotes, but without reference symbols or numbers, paraphrases of lines quoted in French in the text. The equivalents are of meanings, not words:

First, compression—the conveying of the fullest meaning in the fewest syllables. I include under meaning emotion. Clearly, the words and syntax of one language cannot be counted on to effect compression upon a given idea whenever some other language can. Next, poetry in the original text sounds at once natural and strange: the phrasing may be simple but never commonplace. The strangeness comes from combining pregnant terms in uncommon ways. Part of the poetic value lies right there, in the reader's awareness of the words the poet did *not* use. This alone would preclude translation, since the foreign reader's recourse to a paraphrase implies that he lacks that awareness: he cannot sense the degree to which the words sound natural and their collocation strange.

The importance of this point will appear central when we come to the English reader's incomprehension of French poetry. Just as the poetry evaporates when "Absent thee from felicity awhile" is turned into: "Give up your pleasant occupations for a time," so a French verse will sound like a dull paraphrase when read as a sort of translation from an imagined English line.

Finally, poetry embodies one or another kind of harmony. I mean by that hedging phrase whatever audible interest the current poetics call for—meter, quantity, alliteration, assonance, rime, "verbal music," or any combination of these. In translation, much of this harmony vanishes. The rimes are not the same, the rhythm is fitfully simulated within the constraints of a perhaps modified meter, and the "music" is at war with the requirement of meaning—in short, a series of compromises squeezes out most of what made the line poetic.

I now ask whether analyzing the obstacles to translation does not come close to defining poetry: compression, strangeness fused with the natural, and the spell variously put on the ear. I suspect that these elements are what Milton had in mind when he gave his laconic definition "simple, sensuous, and passionate." These characteristics apply, of course, to the verbal substance only; they do not guarantee the merit of *a poem*, which requires in addition a fit theme and structure. But these are more easily assessed, and critics have seldom been baffled by the need to define them.

Now return to the English tradition that A.E. Housman chose to follow in welcoming Gide to Cambridge. Its strength is made clear in John Bailey's brief remark at the head of this section, and as I indicated, its origins go back to the time when England—and indeed all of Europe—turned, for very good reasons, against French Neoclassicism. It had outlived its virtues, and the arrogance with which the French had imposed their culture on other countries had become intolerable. When Lessing, reviewing plays in Hamburg, attacked Voltaire and touted Shakespeare—the year was 1767—he sounded the call to a war of liberation.

Likewise in England, the object of attack was naturally the contemporary French output—Voltaire again—and more particularly the dominant vehicle of French playwriting, the alexandrine line of twelve syllables riming in pairs. Here is Voltaire in a five-act tragedy of 1750:

> Ah! Clytemnestre encor trouble plus mon courage,
> Dans mon coeur déchiré quel douloureux partage!
> As-tu vu dans ses yeux, sur son front interdit,
> Les combats qu'en son âme excitait mon récit?

It is easy to understand how a long succession of such flat-footed lines (and I chose among the best I could find) would exasperate a critic with a good ear and a mind attuned to—say—the Border Ballads that were coming into favor as fresh blooms of native English and Scottish poetry.

But instead of denouncing Voltaire's vague terms, loose texture, obvious filler, and conventional attitudes in place of feeling, the critics assailed the form itself. Edmund Malone, the great Shakespeare scholar, said the alexandrine corresponded to the popular English meter—"A cobbler there was and he lived in a stall." He mistook a line of twelve syllables for one of eleven.° Another critic, discussing word harmony, called the French meter dactylic (long, short, short), whereas, if it is at all describable in these terms, it is anapestic (short, short, long). Such blunders have a long life. Thomas Moore, musician and poet, accepted Malone's opinion and James Russell Lowell quoted both critics with approval, all of them contemptuous of the line they thought they knew how to scan.

The suspicion begins to dawn that these judges, whether or not they "knew French," certainly did not *hear* it. The surmise is confirmed when one samples the still more confident views of the nine-

---

Ah! Clytemnestra shakes my resolve even more. / In my torn-asunder heart, what painful rival claims! / Did you see in her eyes and on her troubled brow / The struggle that my recital caused in her soul? (*Oreste*, III, 7. The speech follows Orestes' first sight of his mother, who does not know who he is and whom he is destined to kill)

teenth-century denigrators. Coming from great critics—De Quincey, Walter Savage Landor, Matthew Arnold—these opinions cannot be shrugged off as casual sallies.

According to De Quincey, the French poets waste on trivial subjects their technical skill in handling words "and hence have no language of passion for the service of poetry."° Landor agrees and offers to take the worst third of Tasso's *Orlando Furioso*—"vile poetry" in his judgment—and show that "it will contain more good poetry than the whole French language."°

As for Arnold, who so greatly admired the French lycée and the works of George Sand, he confesses to finding immense relief in returning to a simple song in Shakespeare "after dealing with French people of genius irresistibly impelled to try and express themselves in verse, launching out into a deep which destiny has sown with so many rocks for them."° This cryptic image needed no explanation for those whose acquaintance with French verse was slight, or who chanced to have read Landor's partly imaginary conversation with the Abbé Delille, a French poet who in the 1790s spent some time in England during his exile. Landor greets him as Housman did Gide, with an assault. He quotes a line from Racine:

Ah! qu'il eût mieux valu, plus sage ou plus heureux

and underlines, in print, all the *u*'s as if even the diphthongs *eu* and *ou* were sounded *u* and the line were a silly tongue-twister. Then he goes after "Your nasal twang, the most disagreeable and disgusting of sounds, being produced by the same means as a stink is rejected, and thus reminding us of one."° What is significant is that he did not hear his own grunts; for English is not free and clear of nasals. They usually come at the end of words and are called continuants, but there they are: *same, shame, done, sun, sing, ring*, and the innumerable *-ing*s that nasalize our verbs to make participles or adjectives.

The remainder of Landor's onslaught is aimed at Boileau's Ode to Louis XIV, which is easily the poet's worst effort, a courtier's performance obviously written *invita Minerva*. But even while deriding the inflated praise of the monarch, Landor shows his imperfect knowledge of meanings and connotations, with the inevitable result that most of the images seem to him absurd.

Ah, far better had it been if, by wisdom or good fortune, . . .

Earlier critics, such as Lord Chesterfield, who knew French far better than Landor, had deplored the limitations set upon poetic diction by the nature of the French vocabulary and the rules of versification. This sound judgment was echoed in the nineteenth century, but often as proof of a disparaging estimate of the entire French people. Coleridge, for instance, assigns to them the domain of "understanding, fancy, and wit," which in his scheme rank below "reason, imagination, and humor," characteristic traits of the British. "Therefore the French wholly unfit for poetry; because [all] is clear in their language."° And Arnold, in a poem, calls France "famed in all great arts, in none supreme."°

The granting or refusal of greatness is of no concern here, except insofar as it seems to have been a consideration in English criticism of French poetry. Certainly the French in the seventeenth and eighteenth centuries deafened the rest of Europe with boasts of *their* greatness in all things, and the retaliation that ensued was deserved on the moral plane. Only, it should not obscure the facts of language and esthetics.

Recapitulated, the charges leveled at French poetry amount to this: an endless series of twelve-syllable lines riming feebly; a preference for abstractions occasionally rising into a *tirade*, which at best is oratory, not poetry; an invariably moral or social subject-matter— not a bird or flower in a thousand lines—all this is but mannered prose etiolated by needlessly arbitrary rules of versification. The heavily Latinized vocabulary lacks immediacy and evocative power, and being sounded without accent yields no rhythm. As there is but one meter, thought and feeling are encased in virtually standardized propositions. How could the poetic imagination, if it ever stirred in a French breast, survive such stifling conditions?

A reader of modern literature would probably counter the challenge with another question: How then were Eliot, Pound, and their followers able to overcome the well-entrenched prejudice and, having recognized genuine poets in Laforgue, Mallarmé, and Rimbaud, claim them as models for their own innovations? The answer is that these French poets of the 1880s not only did not follow the system, but liberated even further an already free and flexible poetics. What the young English and American writers discovered in Paris just before and after the First World War was a variety of works with (seemingly) few of the characteristics impugned by the English critics' negative dogma.

Today, "French poetry" is no longer a self-contradictory phrase, and sheer surprise greets the fact that its existence was ever in doubt. But even here confusion persists, for a silent proviso is attached to the modern opinion: as I put it briefly—no French poetry before Baudelaire. Villon four hundred years earlier, qualifies by exception—he and Baudelaire share a modern mood and Villon's traditional technique is no bar to appreciation. But between these two poles, the void.

That would seem to close the subject. But for anybody with a love of poetry and some curiosity, the question remains, Was the steady devaluation of French poetry for two hundred years justified? If not, then a look at each of the objections in turn might change its bearing and give access to a very large body of true poetry, as well as explain in terms not disparaging to the past, the shift to poetic Modernism in France and elsewhere.

The French language is not well made.
I should have codified it.
—Napoleon in conversation
on St. Helena (1817)

Having impugned the English critics' knowledge of French, some neglected truths about that language are in order. Except for the empirical evidence that millions have spoken and written it, one would say that French is not merely difficult: it is impossible. For the natives themselves it is full of traps—in grammar, vocabulary, and pronunciation. To the educated foreigner, especially the English, it is peculiarly treacherous, because it gives the impression of being fully understood when in fact it is not. The things I am about to point out are no secret, but they are astonishingly overlooked, and their effect on literature—not on poetry alone—seldom comes to the critic's consciousness.

(I am assuming in the reader an elementary knowledge of French. It would clutter the text to translate every simple word—*main, pain, aimer, parler*—and recall that *être* and *avoir* are auxiliaries used with verbs, and *le, la, les* are articles in front of nouns.)

No two languages are closer and farther apart than English and

French. They are close in their mixed history and mutual borrow-ings, and they look close in their vocabularies—thousands of words are spelled exactly or nearly alike. But they are far apart in grammar and idiom and in the meaning of these very thousands of look-alikes. They are farthest apart in turn of thought and, most important, in the way the "same" sounds are uttered.

French is a vowel language: that is the great principle to remember. It has determined several of the "arbitrary rules" complained of and it solves other puzzles. Whoever wants to learn to speak, or simply to read poems in French, must believe this primacy of the vowels and do something about it.* In his famous *Elements of Rhetoric*, Bishop Whately approves the common English advice to speakers: "Take care of the consonants and the vowels will take care of themselves."° In French, the exact opposite is true. The language numbers offi-cially nineteen vowels, but as Valéry remarked, "The French vowels are numerous and distinctly shaded (*très nuancées*)."° There are more than nineteen "shades," most of them essential to meaning, especially the nasals.

For the sake of the verse harmony that so often escapes the foreign ear, I must labor the point. One reason French tradesmen are often impatient with foreigners' speech is not chauvinism, it is frustration: what am I hearing?—*Danton, d'Antin, Autant, Autun?* There is no way to guess. Is the tourist saying *trop loin, trop lent, or trop long?* The taxi-driver's tantrum is despair. Even a completely bilingual ear (as it were) is baffled by this confusion, which Ronald Knox parodied in quoting Musset:

> Qu'est ce que c'est que le tong
> Maintenong?°

French, moreover, never allows a plain vowel to turn indistinct (the linguist's *schwa*), as in the last syllable of "author," the first of

---

Qu'est ce que c'est que le temps / Maintenant? (What is time, now?) The American analogue of this corrupt vowel occurs in "lanjeray" and "chaise lounge" (*lingerie, chaise longue*), which have become virtually standard pro-nunciations.

*Over the years I have recommended to students and friends with a reading knowledge of French that on their first visit to France they enroll in the six-week course at the Institut de Phonétique, where the right sounds are drilled into their vocal apparatus. Invariably, those who took the course came back speaking and understanding French; the others did not. Only by being able to *utter* can one properly *hear*.

"career," the middle one of "emphasis," and a host of others. This vagueness in English is normal, for as Whately said, the consonants suffice. In a typical long word such as "enlightenment" there is only one clear vowel out of four. In French, the failure to differentiate *é* and *è* or any other related pair denatures the word. Take the rough play on words in the title of the comedy *Oh! Calcutta* (*oh! quel cul t'as*); it disappears altogether when the *u* in Calcutta is given its English pronunciation. The English speaker may not be as ignorant as Landor; he is merely unable to say the fluted *u*, the four nasals, and the first syllable *e* of *Monsieur*. "No Englishman," says Uncle Ponderevo in H.G. Wells's *Tono Bungay*, "pronounces French properly." When he tries to, "it's all a bluff." And as if to prove it, he quotes "Le steel say lum."*°

Although the French vowels are farthest from their English analogues, the consonants also differ markedly. As everybody knows, the *r* is difficult, whether one attempts the Parisian near the throat or the southern, trilled on the tongue, both admissible. The *l*-sound is the continental *l*, less fruity and forceful than the English; and the rest, in French alone among European languages, must be toned down and brought out without explosiveness.

There is an old American catchphrase according to which "Paddle your own canoe" is supposedly rendered in French through the (meaningless) sentence: *Pas de lieu Rhône que nous*. On the same erroneous principle, a bilingual writer has published a small volume called *Mots d'heures gousses rames*. Uttered properly, these French words in no way reproduce the intended "Mother Goose Rhymes," and this holds true of the contorted equivalents inside the book.° The consonants in each destroy the resemblance with the other.

French has a distaste for consonants just as English is impatient of vowels. In the early Middle Ages the French used to pronounce *d*'s and *t*'s and *p*'s at the end of words; they have dropped them since, while keeping many of them in the spelling. At the beginning of words, the French of every age have found double consonants hateful and got rid of one or the other at the earliest opportunity: spasmus became *pâmer;* scala, *échelle;* spatha, *épée*. In the middle position, the consonants of the Latin originals were also purged: *nativum* turned into *naïf;* hospitalem, *hôtel;* regem, *roi; potionem, poison*. To these feats must be added the softening of words borrowed from English or

---

* *Le style c'est l'homme*, which is the traditional version of Buffon's actual words: *Le style est l'homme même*. ("Sur le style," *Discours à l'Académie*, 1753)

German: bowling-green = *boulingrin;* packet-boat = *paquebot;* boll-werk = *boulevard;* landsknecht = *lansquenet.* The French are lazy-lipped.

At the same time, the French consonants, though muted as compared with the English, must remain perfectly clear and distinct. It will not do to blur *t*'s and *d*'s or *p*'s and *b*'s as foreigners can do in English and still be understood.

These dampers on vocal energy act as both cause and effect in the well-known lack of what is the main feature of English poetry—a definite stress on some part of each word. In French, a very light stress—no more than a slightly rising tone—lands on the last syllable of the word and on the last word of any unit of meaning—a phrase or sentence. In this lack of accentuation, French, again, is unique among European languages. It resembles (I am told) Algonquin, which after the American War of Independence was proposed in New York as the national replacement of the hated English. But stresslessness was a fatal obstacle to adoption by speakers used to accenting their words. In French, even the weak tonic accent, as it is called, may be neutralized for various reasons and shifted to different syllables. Hence a great variety in poetic rhythm in the very place where the inattentive find monotony.

Knowing these facts will not by itself open the foreign ear to French poetry, but it should at least modify prejudice by holding in check the mistaken impression that the rhythm of verse after verse is drearily the same. Take Hugo's line:

Je suis veuf, je suis seul, et sur moi la nuit tombe

The accents fall on *veuf* and *seul* and not again until *tombe;* but it would be possible in reading aloud to raise the voice a little on *moi,* besides which there are two ways of sounding the final word: *tomb'* and *tomb(eu);* that is, the so-called mute *e* can be neglected or given a slight value. The choice would probably depend on whether the next line opened with a vowel or a consonant, or again, on whether the sense stopped at *tombe* or went on.

What is this mute *e?* It ends many French words, and its role in spelling is to make sure that the preceding consonant is sounded; without the *e,* one would automatically suppress the *b* of *tombe* and pronounce the word like *ton,* just as in *plomb* (the metal "lead") one

---

I am alone, I am bereft and over me darkness is falling.

says *plon*. It is this same *e* that ends many English words in Chaucer, where it must be pronounced if his lines are to scan. Soon after his death English pronunciation changed, the *e* was dropped, and for three centuries his work was neglected as unmetrical doggerel.

In French, mute *e* has a second role, which is to indicate the feminine in adjectives: *clair, claire*. Finally, in verb forms ending in *-ent* (third person plural), these three letters count and are pronounced as a mute *e*. In reality, this *e* is not mute but obscure, toneless. It should also be called unstable, since it can be sounded or not and, as Jeanne Varney Pleasants has shown by delicate measurements, it is sounded by the same or different speakers in widely varying degrees of length and forcefulness.° It might thus seem as if French did have after all a vowel like the English schwa (*uh*). But the two are not comparable, because the mute *e* has definite places and uses, whereas the English *uh* can be put for almost any unstressed vowel anywhere as a means of speeding up utterance. The important conclusion is this: with its strong accent, English comes down hard on one key syllable which is virtually enough to give the meaning of the word; stressless French requires equal value throughout and meaning fails without it.

The combined effect of these peculiarities is nicely illustrated by an anecdote in Heine's reminiscences. After the poet came to Paris as a political refugee in the 1830s, he was sought out by German friends (and spies) who traced him to his successive lodgings. But he was never caught up with, says Heine, because they went about asking the concierges and shopkeepers for one HEINrich HEINe, whereas all these good people knew only of their neighbor *Enryenn*.

I shall have more to say about the language, though with no idea of offering an advanced course in it. It is not so much the details as their bearing that is to be remembered; the indications I give here should bring out what might be called the inner voices that French poets have worked with, and thereby induce a more tentative—and attentive—approach to French poetry.

While pronunciation and accentuation separate the two languages, grammar and vocabulary make them seem close. They are both "analytic" languages, that is, they have dropped most inflections and show grammatical relations by position—subject, verb, predicate. But as hinted earlier, the kinship in vocabulary is a constant cause of deception—hundreds of words visually the same, from identical Latin roots, and possibly carrying the same meaning, but again and again having a sharply divergent use or connotation. Take this common word *deception* I have just used: its counterpart in French implies no deceit, it means disappointment. French grammar is hard enough for the foreign learner; it takes a lifetime of alert reading for the English speaker to make sure he grasps the right connotations of familiar words. Even veteran translators of prose stumble and publish what is not merely false connotations but factual error.

Thus *malice* does not mean malice but mischievousness; *fastidieux* not fastidious but tiresome; an *égoïste* is not an egotist but a selfish person; *une phrase* is not a phrase but a sentence; *atroce* rarely means atrocious: it is usually "cruel"; *demander* is never "demand," but merely "ask"; *prétendu* is not "pretended" but "alleged"; *curé* and *vicaire* must be rendered in reverse order: vicar and curate. As for an *ancien ami*, he is not an old friend but formerly a friend.*

The recurrent small words and transitional phrases are misleading too: *en effet* is not "in effect" but "sure enough"; *mon Dieu!* never means "my God!" and *bien*, which is part of so many expressions, should seldom be rendered "well"—it has a dozen or more other meanings. Several books have been compiled to guide reader or translator amid these perils and the term "false friend" aptly coined to designate the insidious similars. Many idioms seem perversely designed to mislead. The foreigner's reading of French poetry is thus continually threatened. One misconception, one false nuance, one implied feeling overlooked will ruin a line. In a respected version of a Baudelaire poem we come upon "the sainted earth"; it should be simply the Holy Land. The very title *Fleurs du Mal* is twisted slightly out of true by being rendered as Flowers of Evil. For one thing, *fleurs* connotes rather fruits, products; and for another, *du mal* refers not so much to sin as to *the* Evil (principle), Satan himself.

This self-misrepresentation of the French vocabulary is compounded by another characteristic: French is not double like English, but single: it does not possess a second, Latinate word parallel to the Anglo-Saxon derivative—"tool" and "instrument," "strength" and "fortitude," "land" and "territory," "quick" and "rapid," "motherhood" and "maternity." Such pairs are not exact duplicates; usually,

*For good measure, consider some meanings that are more usual than the ostensible ones:

surtout	is often	*especially*		instead of	*above all*
rêver	"	"	*think of, wish for*	"	"	*dream*
monde	"	"	*people, society*	"	"	*world*
aussi	"	"	*and so, therefore*	"	"	*also*
heureux	"	"	*apt, fortunate*	"	"	*happy*

the sense of the Latin derivative is more abstract or lofty. Thus the space ship was named Voyager and not Tripper (or even Traveler), and when Wordsworth wrote of Newton, he spoke of him as *"voyaging* through strange seas of thought." French has only the one word *voyageur*, and the effect of this lack on the unreflecting English is that French poetry seems to be always "aloft," full of fancy words and resounding abstractions—

C'était pendant l'horreur d'une profonde nuit

—why can't Racine say "dread" and "deep"? Because he has Virgil behind him and not *Beowulf.* And the critical mistake is to feel *profonde* as meaning profound when it does mean deep.

So much for semantics. The gap between the two languages grows still wider, if possible, when we take a look at the turn of mind that each embodies. English teachers have made it a platitude to say: style depends on strong verbs; avoid nouns linked with the passive voice and you gain vigor and movement. French style goes the opposite way. It prefers verbs that are as neutral as possible and it throws the emphasis on the noun. Thus: not "frighten" but *faire peur;* not "kick" but *donner un coup de pied;* not "compete" but *entrer en concurrence;* not "cry out" but *pousser des cris;* and so on. A few verbs—*être, avoir, prendre, mettre, donner*—carry on their backs a huge burden of nouns and phrases which express fine discriminations that are by no means self-explaining. They correspond to our prepositional verbs—*give in, out, up, off,* etc., which form the principal difficulty in learning English.

French addiction to nouns appears again in the ease with which verbs and adjectives are made into substantives: *le savoir, le boire et le manger* (meat and drink), *le beau parler* (fine language); and from adjectives: *un pauvre, une bonne, les fous, des poilus.* English works the other way and makes nouns into verbs and adjectives: we *sun* ourselves, the laundry *irons* the shirts; a *music* critic, the *Friday* concert, and so on.

"Turn of mind" means that correct translation is not enough. For example, if you want to say that someone has impeccable manners but is not very friendly, you can give the equivalent of each word in turn and you will be understood, but your sentence will not sound like real French. You must turn the thought and say: *"il est d'une parfaite courtoisie, mais il est peu abordable."*

This desirable change of conception brings us to a last pair of verbal tricks that makes French harder to grasp at sight than other European languages. French avoids the passive voice by means of reflexive verbs that are not reflexive at all but passive in sense: *le plat se mange arrosé de citron* = the dish is served with lemon juice; *ce livre se lit facilement* = the book is easy to read; *on se rencontre tous les jeudis* = the meetings are held every Thursday. To an English poet, this twist in the action may seem a drag on direct expression, but to the French it feels more direct (being active) than all our English passives.

At the same time, French is implacably analytic; it wants relations explicitly stated where English takes them for granted: we say toothbrush and driving license; French must have *brosse à dents* and *permis de conduire.* Even when English consents to spell things out as in "botanical garden," French calls for *jardin des plantes,* because to say *jardin botanique* strikes the analytic mind as contrary to fact: it isn't the garden that's botanical, but solely the methods, terms, and findings of the science of botany.

Under the pressure of technology, world trade and travel, and American-style advertising, French has latterly been swamped by expressions that run counter to these native habits. But these invaders—this Franglais—will not help one to read with intelligence Ronsard or Lamartine or even such a latter-day poet as Jacques Prévert.

The analytical bent has given rise to the belief that French is the most logical of languages. It is nothing of the sort. In many ways it is the most illogical of all European tongues. From spelling to syntax and pronunciation to usage it is a mass of inconsistencies and of difficulties created by historical accretion and want of logic. But French is clear—not more so than other languages, but it shows up lack of clarity at once and painfully. The urge to split hairs over meanings and the interrelations of ideas has made writers so self-critical that for three hundred years prose and verse in French have lived up to the demand for exact naming and precise linking. "Just so," says the hostile critic, and adds: "How can poetry flourish without evocative haze, without a margin of uncertainty in the terms and the connections, so as to free the imagination, instead of shackling it in tight little units of things correctly named?"

I shall answer the question later on. Here another question belongs, which Anglo-American readers of French poetry ask themselves, or should ask: how does a verse in French actually sound? French pronunciation is difficult on two counts. There is the problem of the sounds to be produced; another is to interpret the spelling. Landor was in a fury about French spelling too: "That cannot be a language of which the sounds are reducible to no rules." He did not see that on this score English is bad enough; he only saw that French was worse, and that when the thing at stake is a line of poetry, the defects of spelling can be catastrophic. Consider a few of the endless French anomalies: *six* and *dix* are "siss" and "diss"; this sibilance turns into a *z* before vowels (si-z-hommes) and both sounds disappear before a consonant (si-livres). In *prix* and *perdrix*, *x* is silent, but it is heard as *x* (not *s*) in *lynx* and *sphinx*. *Gaz* sounds final *z*, *riz* does not. *Moëlle* and *poële* are pronounced *moile* and *poile; paon* and *faon, pan* and *fan. Lac* (a lake) is spoken "lak," but *lacs* (snare) is "la"; *ours* with audible *s, cours* without. As for *fils*, it may mean son or sons with the *s*, and threads if the *l* (but no *s*) is heard. But drop that final *l* in *outil* (tool) and recapture it for use in *poil* (hair).

And now, with all your vowels in readiness, pick up a poem and read it so as to get the full sound value that the poet worked hard to bless it with. It is extremely difficult; the conscientious reader, before judging the harmony of a line, will want to settle the doubts he may have about a word by consulting a good pronouncing dictionary.

But it is time to get to that line.

The prevailing meter in English poetry has been the iambic pentameter, blank or rimed, but it would be foolish to think or pretend that other meters have not been abundantly used. The same holds true of the French alexandrine. The critics who attack the French poets by representing them as wedded exclusively to that measure are not excusable even when the objection refers to the century-and-a-half of Neo-classicism. The alexandrine did predominate then, but there were lyricists and satirists at that time who used lines of six, eight, or ten syllables, all traditional in French. Yet the importance of the alexandrine down to this very day calls for a look at its character and the circumstances of its origin and curious development.

Its deliberate use goes back to that immensely creative thirteenth century, although it can be traced to the late eleventh and, faintly, earlier. Throughout this formative period, poetry was still the twin of music. Poets composed in both arts together, or wrote words to tunes already current, and were themselves the performers on some stringed instrument. These "troubadours" of Provence, whom everybody has heard of, were not casual minstrels, but highly conscious poets. They standardized their speech by deliberate artifice and used stanzas made arresting by ever-greater intricacy of rime and sense. Their perennial theme of love often managed to include matters of social interest.

Before their ten-syllable forms inspired the Italian poets who came before Dante, this *poésie courtoise* of southern France had been introduced into the north by Eleanor of Aquitaine in the second half of the twelfth century. There new genres developed—epic, narrative, dramatic—most still tied to music but gradually separating from it. By the fourteenth century some of the verses of Charles d'Orléans are for recitation, and in the fifteenth Villon writes to be read, though still using the once musical patterns. Of these the ballade is a familiar survival in both French and English. In French versification, the final divorce from music had an all-important result: it left but two strong accents in each line, one at the cesura or break, and the other at the end, marked by the rime.

It was this huge written literature of northern France—all in verse—that influenced the rest of Europe, including Germany and the England of Chaucer. One of the most admired as well as most popular works was *Le Roman de la Rose*, by Jean de Meung, of which Chaucer translated a good portion. Nor did his interest stop there. As the *Oxford History of English Literature* puts it in describing his place at the court of Edward III: "Everyone knew that the fountainhead of literature was France: . . . Chaucer found in French a wealth of romances, lives of saints, *contes, fabliaux*, drama, history, biography, all of great interest and importance."°

In the "histories," the fabulous deeds of Aeneas or Brutus, of King Arthur or Tristan were recounted in cantos as entertaining and interminable as soap operas. Each subject was treated again and again by different poets at different times and places. About the year 1225, one such French poet named Alexandre de Bernai (and also de Paris) chose to recast the current *Alexandre* (the Great) from the standard ten-syllable line into lines of twelve syllables. Thus was established, by sheer bulk, the alexandrine, named after its author and his subject, both.

Its success was fitful and not until three hundred years after its first extended use did Ronsard, chief poet of the sixteenth-century *Pléïade*, revive it and give it in French poetry its accomplished form and permanent place. At first Ronsard and his group called themselves a brigade. Later, seven of them were singled out and dubbed *la Pléïade* (in English, Pleiades, after the Greek myth of the seven stars and the constellation of the astronomers). The seven were: Ronsard, Du Bellay, Baïf, Peletier, Belleau, Jodelle, and Pontus de Thyard.* The poems they addressed to each other give an idea of the degree to which they saw themselves as the *avant-garde*, a term first used by their contemporary, the historian Pasquier.° Theirs was an exuberant outpouring of genius bent on making all things new. Poets even tried to write ancient meters in modern languages, replacing the usual syllabic lines by the classical feet in short-and-long vowel patterns. Jacques de la Taille supplied a theory, and in England Spenser and others made the same attempt;° it did not work in either language, "length" being too indeterminate, especially in French.

This French was a language that had greatly changed since *Alexandre*. Whereas Chaucer can be read fairly easily today by whoever knows English and some French, the thirteenth-century *Alexandre* is incomprehensible to modern French readers. Only by the time of Ronsard and Montaigne can they begin, with a little help, to read their own literature. Between those periods, Villon is the one great poet generally known, in either French or English, thanks to brilliant "approximations" of his works by poets of recent date.

What happened to old French was the gradual loss of its inflections, followed by the decimating of its vocabulary when the Renaissance passion for Greek and Latin authors introduced a flood of new words patterned on elements from these languages. The new words came in virtually "raw"—without the whittling and polishing done by popular usage on earlier Latin during the long Middle Ages. I have mentioned the medieval smoothing of *potionem* into *poison;* the Renaissance took the Latin word again and coined *potion*. Similar work with Greek roots brought in the letter *y* (*i-grec*) and the *ph, th,* and other combinations of letters that make French (and English) spelling so inconsistent. One has only to read Rabelais, who both used and made

---

* His name is sometimes replaced by that of Dorat, but the latter was a learned supporter of the movement rather than a contributing poet.

fun of the pedantic creations, to see how swollen with absurd vocables French suddenly became. This enlargement by hasty manufacture caused damage to poetry on two counts, as will appear.

Meantime, Ronsard and his fellows managed to keep a balance between the new and the old and produced a body of work in what begins to be modern French. The bulk of it is by Ronsard himself. A great lover, scholar, and conscious revolutionary in poetry, he lived long and tried all genres—odes, sonnets, elegies, love lyrics, epistles, epigrams—using meters and stanzas of every kind. Coming after the fluent, unassuming Clément Marot, he created the grand style in his *Hymnes* and other long poems, as well as in his love sonnets.

It was for these works that he remolded the alexandrine line. It had been used for run-of-the-mill story-telling; with Ronsard it acquired emotional amplitude and majesty of sound, matching his sense of living in a new world full of light and energy. To make the count of syllables exact, he disallowed the earlier freedom about the mute *e*. Villon could write: *La pluie nous a débués et lavés*, in which the second word has to be thought of as written *plui* if the line is to scan.° Ronsard also called for "rich" rimes, that is, sonorous, not mere assonance. The alexandrine fulfilled his desire to emulate—not copy—the art of the ancients. He often used it to express his love of nature, always associated with personal memories. His elegy on a well-loved wood that was cut down shows this alexandrine mood:

> Plus le cerf solitaire et les chevreuls légers
> Ne paistront sous ton ombre, et ta verte crinière
> Plus du soleil d'Esté ne rompra ta lumière
> . . . .
> Adieu vieille Forest, le jouet de Zéphyre,
> Où premier j'accorday les langues de ma Lyre,
> Où premier j'entendi les flèches résonner
> D'Apollon, qui me vint tout le coeur estonner.

The rain has scoured and rinsed us [the corpses hanging on the roadside gallows] (*Epitaphe en forme de ballade*)

No longer will the solitary deer nor the light-footed roebuck / Browse under your shade, nor your verdant mane / Any longer cut across the light of summer suns /. . . . Farewell, ancient wood, plaything of the winds / Where I first tuned the strings of my lyre, / Where I first heard the hum of the arrows / With which Apollo startled my whole heart. ("Contre les bûcherons de la forêt de Gastine," *Elégies*, XXIV)

Ronsard's alexandrines are regular in that they show a pause in the middle and alternate pairs of masculine and feminine rimes, but they contain features that the next century forbade. This regression was part of an amazing linguistic counter-revolution that had social and political motives as well. Because the sixteenth-century vocabulary was in fact cluttered, overblown, the next generation began a pruning operation that went beyond necessity and caused the double damage I spoke of: the language was impoverished and the poets trammeled. Ronsard was free; Racine was hemmed in.

In the French lycée of modern times, there is a passage from Boileau's *Art Poétique* that is drilled into the students' unwilling memories:

> Enfin Malherbe vint et le premier en France
> Fit sentir dans les vers une juste cadence

The idea is that until that good but limited poet Malherbe came along in the year 1600, French poetry was nothing but extravagance and carelessness. This kind of overturn is a common occurrence in the history of culture. The sons are sure the fathers did not know what they were doing or ought to do, and the grandsons, without investigating, take the judgment as gospel. Thus were Ronsard and his train obliterated for nearly three hundred years. Those who took their place were Malherbe and a few other poets and prose writers, seconded by a coterie of titled ladies who prided themselves on delicacy of taste. These were the "Précieuses" whom Molière later ridiculed for the excess of zeal that led them into absurd circumlocution. In their day they fostered a desirable "purification" on several levels, for the manners as well as the speech of the aristocracy were still clumsy and coarse. When the surgery on French diction was done, Boileau complacently summed it up in the couplet above.

At long last Malherbe appeared / And first in France imposed on verse due measure.

This summary disposal of the whole Renaissance was not the work of the fickle French alone. About the same time as Boileau, an English critic was writing: "Mr. Waller was indeed the parent of English poetry, and the first that showed us our tongue had numbers and beauty in it." (Francis Atterbury, Preface to Waller's [posthumous] *Poems*, London, 1690) Evidently, Marlowe, Shakespeare, Spenser were bunglers.

Malherbe's *juste cadence* governed the alexandrine. It required the following: the break (cesura) must come exactly in the middle; that is, each half line must make up a complete unit of meaning; the whole line must also be self-contained—no runover, such as is found in the last couplet I quoted from Ronsard, where *D'Apollon* belongs in sense to the previous verse and adds a second pause before the cesura. Even the second half of line two, though regular enough, leans toward the third line rather than completes the meaning of its own first half. In short, Ronsard fashioned within the meter a rhythmic pattern, graced by variety, that follows the movement of his thought.

The new rules for pause and rime were limiting enough; they were only the beginning, for at the same time the linguistic reforms dictated by the Précieuses and their favorite oracle, Vaugelas, determined for some two centuries what is and is not French. There is no denying that usage was chaotic. Educated persons would as soon say *j'avons* or *j'étons* as *j'ai* and *je suis;* the Graeco-Latin compounds were being *mis*used and the older, clear and simple words were getting blurred in sense. Ronsard, for all his innovative fervor, had spoken up for them and worried about the poor assimilation of the novelties, but he had other things to do than be a grammarian.

When the pruning squad went to work, they were aided by a widespread desire to establish standards, to unify and centralize: a new King was on the throne and all longed for stability after a time of troubles close to civil war. Thus was the dogma established that for any purpose only one word, one mode of phrasing was right. Add snobbishness to the zeal for order, and you see how the speech of the Court (which the Town would strive to copy) turned out elegant and uniform but trimmed bare and wedded to the cliché. A famous anecdote of the time gives the tone: a piece of writing having been shown to an "illustrious personage," this arbiter of taste smiled and said: "These words must be greatly astonished to find themselves together, for assuredly they had never met before."°

The life in public that goes with monarchy and courtiership reinforced the taste for elegance and the care to avoid shock—in a word, for etiquette. From all these causes a new poetic diction arose; only "noble" words were fit for verse. Those in daily use for the same objects or ideas were "low," good only for practical life and the common people. Where no elegant term existed, the thing itself must not be mentioned, except in roundabout ways. Poets were forbidden to tell the time; if they wanted to say "noon," it had to be: "Phoebus's

chariot has run half its daily course." So the freshly pruned vocabu-
lary was again cut in half. Special prohibitions multiplied: the word
for church was not to be used on the stage, because theatre and sin
were connected—though the tragic muse was in highest honor and
demand. Instead of *église* the playwrights said *temple*, despite its
association with the pagan and the protestant religions.

There were reasons for all this self-denial—or at least the acts were
rationalized. Public opinion held that France was entering a new age,
creating a high civilization at last. Poets, and especially dramatists,
might represent passion and conflict, but the life they depicted must
appear cleansed not merely of grossness but of commonplace detail.
The passions would then be clearly seen in their essence. For this
purpose it was wise to attribute them to figures drawn from ancient
Rome and Greece, after stripping these of all local color. Only
comedy could make use, sparingly, of the colloquial and contempo-
rary. The sudden drop in tone caused laughter, as Molière knew—
and he was blamed for letting the device corrupt his diction.

This standardization of literature became such a familiar fact that
by the middle of the next century it led Thomas Gray (him of the
Elegy) to believe that of all the European tongues French was the only
one in which the language of conversation and of poetry was one and
the same; therefore French poets, unlike the English, got no help
from archaic and obsolescent terms that lend color and strangeness. °
Gray was an excellent student of both French and the history of
poetry in Europe, but he apparently did not perceive the "strange-
ness" imparted by the "noble" vocabulary.

On top of the constraints imposed by the new code of verse
construction, another set came from the make-up of French itself. Its
being a vowel language precluded what is technically called hiatus. A
hiatus or "yawning" occurs when two vowels have to be uttered in
succession: we say "a*n* accident" because "*a* accident" forms a
hiatus—"hiccup" or "stutter" would describe it better than "yawn-
ing." In French, hiatus can be avoided only by elision or by liaison.
Eliding one vowel—saying *l'*arbre instead of *le* arbre—gets rid of the
hiatus, and so does liaison, which activates a consonant or throws one
in: the *t* in *y a-t-il* or the *s* in m*es*-(z)-*a*mis instead of the normal *mè*, as in
mes livres. All mute *e*'s can be elided and all nasals make liaisons: *un*-
n-animal, *en*-n-avant. But this leaves many common expressions
incurable by these means and thus excluded from Neo-classic verse:
tu as, tu es, il y a, si on veut, joli oiseau, peu à peu, j'ai été, and so on. *Oui*

would be banned altogether if it were not considered, plausibly enough, as beginning with a consonant.

Hiatuses vary in badness: *il y a* and *tu es* are not nearly so awkward to say as *et après* or *a acheté*, which nobody would plead for. Yet all are forbidden alike, a severe handicap for the versifier, since it kills in the egg any number of ideas that come spontaneously to mind as natural or striking. And changes in habits of speech add to the predicament. At some point in the nineteenth century, words ending in *-er* (pronounced like *é*) no longer sounded the *r* in liaison with a vowel. Racine could write, with a perceptible *r:*

> Rendre docile au frein un coursi*er in*dompté

Two hundred years later, a poet would not risk the *-ier-(é)-in* hiatus brought about by changed habits of speech.

This example reminds us that the nasals *in, un, an, on*, are vowels indeed. They will clash with their own kind, as much as with the plain ones, whenever the final *n* cannot make liaison with what follows. *Un chagrin inquiet* is a deplorable sequence—though Racine wrote it. *En Amérique* can sound the *n* before *a* and is licit, but *en Hongrie* is ruled out, because the *h*, technically aspirate, bars elision and liaison both. What a language! If the nasal vowel precedes a plain one, it is a matter of tact whether the collocation will escape censure; a pause in the sense will ease the pain; but if the sense is continuous, the hiatus will be noticeable, as in another of Racine's verses:

> Le dess*ein en* est pris. Je pars, cher Théramène.

A word more about liaisons: some are dangerous, as in Laclos' famous novel. First, a poet must know how to handle aspirated *h*. There *is* no aspirated *h* in French, but some words that begin with *h* are deemed to have this invariably silent letter aspirate. Others are not. In *les hommes* one says *lay-zom;* but in *les haricots* the *h* is as it were activated: one must say *lay-arrico*, and this second pair contains a hiatus. Besides the *h*-question, there are certain words such as *onze* that cannot tolerate liaison and still others that cannot make up their

---

Train to heed the bridle an untamed steed.

My mind is made up. I am leaving, dear Théramène.

minds. They accept the tie in some places and not in others, depending on the entire succession of sounds. Thus poets have argued that the phrase *loin encore* was proper in verse, even though *loin-n-encore* would sound affected in conversation.

In fact, modern speech has tended to give up making liaisons other than with *s* and *t*, and even some of these drop out in familiar talk. To put in all possible liaisons suggests great formality—or controlled anger. In applying for a high position or in denouncing an opponent, liaisons rise to the lips as a weapon in the tense encounter. Of course, a few traditional ones have the force of idiom: *pied-à-terre*, with the *d* sounded as *t* and *sang et eau*, with the *g* rendered as *k*, are compulsory. But in *le pied à l'étrier* or in *rang honorable* and similar sequences the *d* and *g* remain silent and hiatus occurs.

The Neo-classical poet's last point to settle in writing his verse has to do with diphthongs. The count of syllables in words that end, for example, in *-ion* is not fixed. In *Cyrano de Bergerac* one finds:

> Pension paternelle, en un jour tu vécus

If spoken on the street, this verse would have only eleven syllables, the first word being uttered in two syllables: *pen-sion*. But Rostand quite legitimately made it three: *pen-si-on*, and it is anybody's guess whether an actor in the role will deliver the line short or long. Endless argument has gone on as to which words containing diphthongs can stand the distortion without sounding ridiculous, and long lists have been made of those eligible for lengthening. Obviously, *ciel* and *cieux* can only be one syllable, the *e* and *eu* being short and the whole word spoken at one stroke. But what of *précieux*, where the length of the word somehow makes *ci-eux* plausible? *Pieux* can stand the same treatment, but *vieux* cannot—why not? Because the word is so commonly used. French "vowelness" exacts a high price! In the event, poets have followed their instinct more often than they have consulted the lists, for the lengthening often contributes to the harmony of the line. Only, the poet depends on the reader to scan the verse correctly in his mind's ear; it needs its full count of syllables—for example, in Hugo:

> C'était l'heure tranquille où les *li-ons* vont boire

Fatherly allowance, you lasted but a day.

It was the quiet time when the lions slake their thirst.

With this example we may leave the French vowels to shift for themselves and come to the versifier's last hurdle, the consonants. The thought occurs that since these limit riming, and do so not according to sound, but to looks, it is convenient to set down first what rime is in French; in the course of it the rules about consonants will be clearly seen for what they are—an historical encumbrance.

IV

> Rime is but a parvenu pun.
> —Victor Hugo

Whereas quite a few English poets have deplored or rejected the use of rime, most French ones have thought it indispensable. One of the greatest masters of versification, Théodore de Banville, wrote in 1871 a small treatise on the art, in which he declared that rime was the source of all melody, harmony, and structure, of artistic rigor and intellectual power.° A generation before him, Sainte-Beuve had expressed the same conviction in fewer words:

> Rime, l'unique harmonie
> Du vers, qui sans tes accents
> Frémissants
> Serait muet au génie.

It is clear that these two poet-theorists meant by rime something that goes beyond coupling "moon" and "June" and torturing the brain to bring them plausibly together. Banville believed that the genuine poet conceives almost at a stroke a series of rimes in a given order which, even if incomplete, determines the meaning, tone, color, and form of the poem. The non-poet, he says, goes at his task the other way, with a subject, which he then tries to outfit with rimes by main force.

Sole harmony of verse, Rime, / Without thy vibrating tones / A line would be but mute / In spite of genius. ("*A la rime*," *Poésies de Joseph Delorme*, 1829)

In English I use the old spelling *rime*, not because it is in fact more correct, but because the continual shifting from French *ri* to English *rhy* would be annoying to read.

Banville's seeming paradox amounts to the modern cliché that poetry is made with words, not ideas. This doctrine Boileau would not have rejected. Addressing Molière, he suggests that rime seems to seek out his friend and confesses himself often unsought:

> Enseigne moi, Molière où tu trouves la rime:
> Dans ce rude métier ou mon esprit se tue,
> En vain pour la trouver je travaille et je sue.

What then are the demands that Boileau rightly felt Molière able to fulfill with ease? French rimes are of several kinds, called *feeble, sufficient, rich, Norman*, and "licentious"—a motley terminology. There are, morever, some nameless conventions to be observed, such as those related to spelling. Because the alexandrine restricts the sense to one line at a time—no runover—it follows that the strongest accent in each line falls on the last syllable. Hence the word at the end that provides the rime must be clear, which for French means a vowel sound, identical, of course, in the two lines that are to rime. The least such sound is that of a solitary vowel—*beauté* and *parlé* make a rime, but it is feeble or *pauvre* (which does not mean poor in the English sense). A better sort, the sufficient, provides more resonance before or after the vowel, as in *fier* and *hier*, *effort* and *transport*, *sommeil* and *pareil*. In this last pair the vowel is double (*ei*) but the sound is still single.

To create a "rich" rime, the consonant(s) preceding the vowels must be alike: *sommeil* and *vermeil*, *armant* and *charmant*. A rime is still richer when the two words sound exactly alike: *bois* (wood) and (*je*) *bois* (drink). In English, this total sameness would make it no rime at all; in French, it is felt as agreeably surprising in its juxtaposition of remote ideas—which is what Victor Hugo implies by calling it a jumped-up pun. The French ear is just as forcibly struck by this *consonne d'appui* or "buttressing consonant" as the English ear is by the required difference in the two consonants: "trace" and "place." In English, "do" and "true" fully satisfy; in French, *doux* and *trous* make only a passable *rime suffisante*.

Seeing all this made Landor burst out and lay down the law: "Rhyme consists in similarity of sound, not in identity—an observation that has escaped all your [French] poets, and what is more

---

Teach me, Molière, where you find your rimes: / In that gruelling, brain-destroying task/ I toil in vain and I sweat blood. (*Satire II: A M. de Molière*)

wonderful, all the Italian."° This last thought should have given him pause. The character of a language conditions the character of its rimes.

Now for the conventions. Strictly viewed, the only thing that matters for rime as sound is the vowel, but the Neo-classical system dictates that riming words must end with the same letter or its equivalent, even though that letter is silent. Thus in masculine pairs, it is illicit to rime *près* and *prêt*, and in feminine *faites* and *nette*. This second pair must either shed or acquire an *s*. By equivalents are meant *d* and *t*; *s*, *x*, and *z*; and *c*, *g*, and *q*. Hence *poids* and *toits* will rime, *pris* and *prix*, *bancs* and *rangs*, and so on.

This last turn of the screw was the result of excessive respect for the past, when final consonants at the end of a line did sound if the following line began with a vowel. In other words, the practice of poetry when sung entailed *liaison* between lines, and when no longer sung the potential liaison was retained for the eye. Fortunately, final *s* or *x* can ease the situation. Thus the adverb *dedans*, which could not rime with *dent*, is allowable with *dents;* other consonants (except *r*) are likewise "covered" by being encased in a plural.

A further excuse for the game with consonants can be found in the fact that to this day many French words must be learned one at a time in order to know whether the final consonant is sounded: one says our*s* but *cour*(s); *oeuf* with *f* in the singular, *oeufs* without it (*eu*) in the plural. And individuals vary: one hears *cerff* as well as the older *cer*, and again, *serf*(f) more often than *ser*. It is these uncertainties that occasion the *rime normande* and the several *licences*. The former has mainly to do with verbs in -*er*, which in standard French sounds like *é*, but which poets occasionally rime with *mer* or *cher*. Here the ear takes its revenge upon the eye.

The other permitted irregularities concern the riming of short vowels with long. The difference is great between *pâte* and *patte*, for *a*, *e*, and *o* can be pronounced short or long. Words with such vowels of different length do not really rime. But *i*, *u*, and *ou* conceal their length from the ear, so that *flûte* and *butte*, *tout* and *goût* make good rimes. The trouble is that certain words occupy a large place in poets' thoughts and must come together occasionally. A license therefore obtains for pairing *âme* and *drame*, as well as for others, notably *même*. This latitude does not extend very far; Hugo was blamed for riming *mai* with *j'aimai*, because this verb ending is (or used to be) sounded *é*, not *è*.°

When such rimes are actually spoken so as to sound alike, either by shortening one vowel or by lengthening the other, the result is comical. One of the brilliant parodies in *A la manière de* makes use of this fact. In a sonnet supposedly by Heredia, the Atlantic cable is gazed at by the neighboring fish. To them, the *câble* is *ce long serpent inexplicâble*, this last word being for the occasion spelled with a circumflex to lengthen the *a* and make the rime exact.° In English, comparable mispronunciations rarely produce humor: *head* and *punishèd* are heard on the Shakespearean stage; and in the mind's ear *none* and *motiön* pass muster without ridicule.

If the great French poets had obeyed all the rules, their range of expression would have been short indeed. But they stretched their bonds as needed. They wrote *encor*(e) to avoid an interfering mute *e*, they rimed *foi* and je *voi*(s) by spelling it in the old way, without *s;* they forgot the audible *s* to make *ours* go with *toujours*, and so on. In the seventeenth century, Molière is the great free-wheeler in this respect, with La Fontaine a close second. And in reading them, one soon discovers that deviation from rule is a source of relief from monotony; the poet could have coerced himself to avoid a fault but wisely preferred to have his say.

Not that the French vocabulary, even in its decanted state, is stingy with rimes. The ubiquitous vowel element makes for a greater choice than English, where the supply tends to be restricted to monosyllables. A scholar has estimated that out of twenty-five thousand English words, nine thousand have different endings, so that any one word finds not quite two others to rime with it.° This paucity brings about couplings that would horrify a French Landor if there were one: *scorn* and *dawn, blood* and *food, reason* and *teazing, curse* and *furze, valley* and *melancholy, bread* and *humbled*—all to be found in Blake. Nor is Pope the classicist much choosier: cries / noise, care / war, appear / reward, break / crack, fool / cowl, outweighs / huzzas, chariots / garrets, Corneille / Ozell.

At the same time, the lordly slurring of vowels in English permits composite rimes of two or more syllables—monotony / got any, blunder / stunned her, random / land 'em, Attic all / mathematical. This ingenuity opens up the unlimited word-play out of which Byron's *Don Juan*, Gilbert's operettas, and a great treasury of light verse were created. No comparable domain exists for the French, who must get along without such things as limericks and clerihews. Banville alone tried to rime English-fashion with humorous intent, and his success exhausted the means the language afforded.

Taken together, the classic rules and conventions of versification in French produce recurrent obstacles that go beyond their separate interference. In the alexandrine particularly, with its compulsory break "down the back like broiled mackerel," said Landor, certain sequences are forever excluded: all common expressions that contain a hiatus; all words that might cause a rime between the sixth syllable and the later or previous twelfth; all words at the cesura that end in a mute *e* before a following consonant, the reason for this last being the need for a strong beat at mid-line. Mute *e* means not only the *-ent* or *ée* of verb forms, but also nouns like *pensée* or *musée*, in which the second *e* does not bear even the slight murmur that is heard in, say, *claire fontaine*.

To sum up the salient points of the system, a few lines will serve. They are from Boileau, as a guarantee of orthodoxy:

> Dans le réduit obscur   d'une alcôve enfoncée
> S'élève un lit de plume   à grand frais amassée:
> Quatre rideaux pompeux,   par un double contour,
> En défendent l'entrée   à la clarté du jour.
> Là, parmi les douceurs   d'un tranquille silence,
> Règne sur le duvet   une heureuse indolence:
> C'est là que le prélat,   muni d'un déjeûner
> Dormant d'un léger somme   attendait le dîner.

The spaces in each line show the cesura, regular as clockwork. The lines begin, two by two, with feminine rimes—all end in mute *e*—and alternate with masculine. The count of syllables is twelve for these and thirteen for the others—or twelve and a half if to your ear mute *e* seems less than a full beat. In the second line, at the end of the first word, occurs an elision between the final *e* of *s'élève* and the opening vowel of *un*. At the cesura (sixth syllable), *plume* would fail to provide the needed accentuation if the next word began with a consonant. But again, *à* lets the *e* of *plume* elide, so that we hear the strong *plum'* and not *plum-uh*. Indeed, what we hear is something like *plumm'//agrand*. In line four the second word, *défendent*, is spoken as if it ended in a

---

In the darkened alcove of a secluded room / There stands a featherbed at great expense acquired. / Four handsome curtains, covering it all around, / Prevent any penetration by the light of day. / There, amid the comforts of unbroken silence / Lies on the downy couch the very bliss of indolence: / There our prelate, fortified by a good luncheon / And enjoying a light slumber, peacefully awaits his dinner. (*Le Lutrin*, Canto I)

mute *e;* the consonants only show the third person plural of the verb.

So much for elision. Now for hiatus. To the man in the street, it might be a question whether in line one *réduit obscur* does not amount to *hiatus.* Technically, no, because the *t* comes between the vowels fore and aft; in reading aloud that *t* would certainly be sounded, though not in colloquial talk. But in line six, at the cesura, the reciter might well omit the liaison between *duvet* and *une,* because the pause at the half line eliminates the "stutter" of *e-u,* akin to saying "a umbrella."

The quality of the rimes in this satirical passage is predominantly "rich"—*enfon*CÉE / *ama*SSÉE, *si*LENCE / *indo*LENCE, *déjeû*NER / *dî*NER all have the "buttressing consonant" preceding an identical vowel. *Jour* and *tour* are "sufficient" rimes, and no odd spelling or pronunciation calls for *licence* of any kind. Nor is there an example of compliance with the visual requirement I detailed. To illustrate it, I need only list a few such rimes that Boileau uses nearby: *bords / efforts, rivaux / dévôts, paix / palais.* The points are that *t* and *d* are licit, *au* and *ôt* are allowed to pair by being covered thanks to *x* and *s;* and *d* and *t, x* and *s* are taken as equivalent in turn.

The features of the language and the prosody—mute *e,* slight stress, consonants smoothed out or ignored, elision, and the exclusion of hiatus—give the line a fluidity that is perceived as speed. The result is that the French twelve syllables seem no longer than the English ten and often give the impression of being shorter. Compare a couplet by Malherbe—

> Les vertus reviendront de palmes couronnées,
> Et ses justes faveurs au mérite données

with one of Dryden's smoothest and swiftest:

> The people's prayer, the glad diviner's theme,
> The young men's vision and the old men's dream.

In an English phrase or sentence the number of consonants causes minute "stops" and no amount of poetic skill can lessen their effect; most of the words keep their separateness, whereas in French, as

---

Virtues will return crowned with palms / And merit receive its just share of favor (*Prière pour le roi*).

The Dryden lines are from *Absalom and Achitophel,* Part I.

someone remarked, no difference is heard between *les petits poissons rouges* and *les petits pois sont rouges.*

In all this, as in all human arrangements, description is more formidable than the reality. During almost a century French writers of verse were able to adapt their thoughts to these stringent demands, and half a dozen among them produced great poetry—poetry that was by no means all of the same kind. Each master had his own voice; none were insensible to what their contemporaries called harmony. Where—or how—this quality found room, few English critics have understood; the disposition of words seems so cut-and-dried, the vocabulary so predictable. As Gray said, no archaisms are permitted, and the supply of noble words, one for each idea, is bound to confine expression within the narrowest of circles.

Corneille was the first of these great poets; he established the language and the form that became the model of tragedy for nearly two hundred years. He was influenced by the Spanish plays of heroism, but created a type of hero and heroine less grandiloquent than his models, though equally devoted to honor, patriotic duty, and religious faith. When Charles Péguy, just before the First World War, said, "We are all Cornelians today," he was referring to the nobility of speech and the image of fortitude that French schools in teaching Corneille held up as sublime. An example of his vigor, and of the emotional stress in his tragedies, is that of Camille, sister to a Roman hero and betrothed to a knight of Rome's enemy Alba. At one point she challenges both his love and his resolve to fight her brother:

> Il faut bien que je pleure;
> Mon insensible amant ordonne que je meure,
> Et quand l'hymen pour nous allume son flambeau,
> Il l'éteint de sa main pour m'ouvrir le tombeau.
> Ce coeur impitoyable à ma perte s'obstine,
> Et dit qu'il m'aime encore alors qu'il m'assassine.

In spite of their respect for the new order, Corneille and his peers did not escape censure. The French critics of the time further

---

How should I not weep? / My heartless lover has decreed that I should die, / For when the rite of love has set alight its flame for us / He snuffs it out and opens my way to the grave. / His pitiless heart is bent on my destruction / And even as he speaks of love, he compasses my murder. (*Horace*, Act II, sc. 5)

shortened the leash by objecting to the slightest deviation from usage, holding it to be a serious fault—criticism then was mostly fault-finding, and it did not let up. A century after Corneille, Voltaire pounces on his diction and imagery, and D'Olivet jibs at Racine's idioms: "Nothing is more usual [in him] than the use of the preposition *de* to mean *avec* or *par*. In some places it seems—at least today—rather a barbarism."° Clearly, the acknowledged genius of an author, his title of classic, his death, and the passage of time did not stop the carping.

But it is instructive. The rebuttal to the demonstration that French Neo-classical rules and poetry were incompatible is that the true poets did as they pleased whenever they wanted. It is simply not true that their work followed the prescription as it is set down on paper. Rather, they adopted the scheme *on the whole* for the support it gave them, and because it had become the accepted means of communication with the public; but they freely flouted its commands. The indictment rendered in England thus seems a compound of imperfect knowledge of French with excessive attention to the rules, instead of to their handling in practice.

Nor is it true that the French poets and their hearers and readers were deaf to "harmony." They relished it, like others before and after them, according to their conception of it, which is not necessarily ours. That is what Gide pointed out. Poetry is not a constant; there are poetries just as there are musics.

Racine was perhaps the most obedient of the Neo-classicists, and as many think, the most perfect. Robert Lowell, who translated *Phèdre*, calls him "perhaps the greatest of French poets; Racine's verse has a diamond edge."° It has—and something more. A characteristic passage will show at once the way Racine bent the rules and the way he achieved harmony, his own:

> Excité d'un désir curieux,
> Cette nuit je l'ai vue arriver en ces lieux,
> Triste, levant au ciel ses yeux mouillés de larmes,
> Qui brillaient au travers des flambeaux et des armes;
> Belle, sans ornements, dans le simple appareil
> D'une beauté qu'on vient d'arracher au sommeil.

Stirred by a strange desire, / Tonight I saw her come into this place / Sad, raising to heaven her tear-filled eyes, / Which shone through the torchlight and the weapons' gleam / Beautiful in the simple unadorned dress / Of a fair creature suddenly roused from sleep. (*Britannicus*, II, 2)

The passage begins with a clear disregard of the cesura: another character has just spoken: *Vous l'aimez?* which enables Nero (and Racine) to utter nine—not six—syllables without a break. Dialogue permits this pleasing irregularity. In line two, the cesura comes after *vue*, of which the *e* makes elision with the *a* of *arriver*. But this exposes a hiatus between the *u* sound and that same *a;* it just gets by because of the slight pause occasioned by the cesura. Line three shows a further means of variety by having the first word cut off in sense from the rest of the line, as well as separated by the slight pause at the mute *e.* The result is that one reads the next eight words all in one breath— another variation from the 6-6 syllabic sing-song. And the headlong effect is repeated at still greater length in the next line, where at the cesura *au travers*, being a preposition, cannot be felt as cut off from its objects, *flambeaux* and *armes*. Still bent on having his own way in designing this vignette of diffused beauty and mysterious confusion, Racine repeats the pattern in the last two lines, where *Belle* corresponds to *Triste* above, with the rest of the line and the next to be read without pause. The scene carries out the theme set in the opening word *excité*, for it goes on through four more lines, of which only the last two restore order by regularity:

> Que veux-tu? Je ne sais si cette négligence,
> Les ombres, les flambeaux, les cris et le silence,
> Et le farouche aspect de ses fiers ravisseurs,
> Relevaient de ses yeux les timides douceurs.

The reader in whom the French language makes no due sound must take it on my say-so that the diction throughout is harmonious in the highest degree. It would be easy to point out where the secondary accents fall that give fluid variety to the ten lines, how the rimes, though only two are rich, are yet sonorous, and why the words convey the grace and strength appropriate to the passing tenderness of the odious character who speaks them. But even the aphonic reader can see that *Que veux tu?* defies the obsession with "noble" expression. Until the final couplet the sway of castiron rule is in abeyance.

The greatest source of freedom for harmony in the French poetry of any period is the variable accentuation that is characteristic of the language. On this point an episode of modern times is instructive. In

---

Can you blame me?—perhaps it was her casual attire / The shadows, the torches, the noise amid the stillness / And the fierce looks of those who had seized her / All heightened the shy sweetness of her eyes.

1905, Richard Strauss wanted to set *Salome* in Wilde's version, which is in French. Strauss applied to his friend Romain Rolland for help, asking questions and submitting his sketches for correction. Rolland was unable, in letter after letter, to teach Strauss how to avoid misplacing the musical accents. "What you call 'unconcern about declamation' is flexibility and psychological truth. We haven't got just one way of stressing a word every time; it is stressed differently according to the meaning and even more according to the character of the speaker."° In short, there is no system. One has to know the spoken language, or else get a Romain Rolland to go over each phrase.

We are told that Racine wanted his actors to chant the lines rather than flatten them to the tone of conversation. (Molière wanted the opposite for his comedies.) So we may infer that the tradition of joining poetry and music had not yet come altogether to an end. At the same time, the theatrical need to make character and conflict convincing suggested that the cesura, and even more, the rimes, should not be too emphatic—sufficient rimes would be preferable to rich, and a dozen ways must be found to "cheat" the mid-line pause into insignificance.

It is this very artfulness that has lent color to the objection that the long speeches in French tragedy are rhetoric, that is, oratory. They are indeed written to be sayable, and like an oration rather than like dialogue. But is this not true of all long speeches on the stage—in Shakespeare and Shaw no less that in Racine and Corneille?

The difference that one notes in Shakespeare is that he mingles lyricism (and comedy) with his tragic harangues. This mixture the French denied themselves. They kept saying they were following the perfect Greek model. But from that model they dropped the elaborate chorus so as to be more intensely dramatic, single-minded in the pursuit of human character. Thus no call for lyrics was made upon these purely tragic writers. The few exceptions to this generality that are found in Corneille and Racine show the non-lyrical nature of their genius.

Whether it was lack of demand or of supply, the French seventeenth century had no lyricist equal to Ronsard, or even to his less fertile companions. Not that after them everybody wrote tragedies like Corneille, Racine, Pradon, Benserade, and others down to Voltaire. There is on the contrary a body of seventeenth-century verse in short forms that has gained in reputation during the last half century. It deals with love, religious faith, courtly occasions, and public affairs, and its best practitioners, like their English Restoration counterparts, are accomplished poets who shine by elegance and wit and management of form, rather than by imagination and passion.°

In comedy, the two giants are of course Molière and La Fontaine. It is La Fontaine himself who called his Fables

> Une ample comédie à cent actes divers
> Et dont la scène est l'univers.

As to Molière, I am among those who think he was a born poet and not merely a comic genius who rimed his scenes to please a verse-mad public. Gladstone thought Molière was a maker of "third-class plays," while other English critics grant him the most comprehensive knowledge of human motives but deny his lines any poetic feature except rime. What they overlook is the mastery of an amazing, unrestricted vocabulary and the poetic qualities of compression, naturalness, and sayability. The mania for wanting the lyric note always and everywhere has abated in recent times; it is now possible to "hear" Molière again and discover his expressiveness through rhythm, imagery, and riming virtuosity. Take the lines

> Vos discours éternels de sagesse et d'honneur,
> Vos mines et vos cris aux ombres d'indécence
> Que d'un mot ambigu peut avoir l'innocence,
> . . . .
> Tout cela . . . fut blâmé d'un commun sentiment.

The phrase *aux ombres d'indécence* is a wonderful *raccourci* through a

---

A vast comedy in a hundred acts / The scene of which is the wide world. ("Le Bûcheron et Mercure," *Fables*, V, 1). Note that the poet's use of "comedy" is like Dante's and means "stage play." An even stricter usage prevailed among some speakers. According to Bouhours, one should say "the comedies of M. Corneille, of M. Racine. Only when performed in a college should the word tragedy be used." (Génin, *Des Variations du langage français*, Paris, 1845, 69)

Your endless speeches about honor and good behavior / Your faces and outcries at a shadow of indecency / Such as innocence may through ambiguity create. . . . / All this by common consent was reproved. (Célimène in *Le Misanthrope*, III, 5)

figure of speech; it defines a character in three words at the start of a portrait which describes action as well, and contrasts the prudish and the innocent. The last line punctures the prude's affectation by the colloquial rhythm of public opinion, anonymous but also judicious.

Except in a few early works, Molière paid no attention to the *précieuses* restrictions. His vocabulary ranges from the current colloquial to the elevated charged with emotion, and not only does it include many of the old, short, expressive words banned by the new order, it also uses the poet's freedom to bend usage to his will within the limits of intelligibility. He makes *à*, *y*, and *où* equivalent, uses adjectives as adverbs, and forces prepositions to obey his feeling for emphasis regardless of what Town and Court might think.

For it was they who by the early eighteenth century had desiccated French poetry in the interests of French prose. They wanted verse to speak the language of polite conversation—no skipping or switching of small words; no inversions except of one sort, as inconspicuous as possible; above all, no words high or low which, by arresting attention as unusual, could halt for an instant the course of understanding. When Molière stretched *humanité* from meaning humaneness to meaning also humankind, it fluttered the dovecotes: the aim of art was transparency achieved by standardized diction. This required that convention be made absolute; it was also to confuse poetry with discourse and reduce form to formality.

But Molière escaped the net, in form as well as in diction. He wrote what his century called *vers libres* in *Le Sicilien* and *Amphitryon*, as well as other irregular measures in his pastorals and ballets. *Vers libres*, in his day, meant lines of varying lengths that rimed together in no set order, though often in alternation of single, not paired lines. Thus in *Amphitryon* Mercury speaks to Sosie, the servant whose likeness he has assumed to serve Jupiter's intrigue:

> Mais de s'en consoler il a maintenant lieu;
> Et les coups de bâton d'un dieu
> Font honneur à qui les endure.

> SOSIE
> Ma foi, monsieur le dieu, je suis votre valet:
> Je me serais passé de votre courtoisie.

―――――――

But now he can console himself: / A beating delivered by a god / Does honor to the recipient. SOSIE: I must say, Mister God, I am indeed your servant / But I could have done without your courtesies. (III, 10)

These liberties did not pass uncensured. Even his good friend Boileau and his admirer La Bruyère "deplored" and "regretted" the use *in Paris* of that inclusive vocabulary he had acquired in his years of itinerant playing in the provinces—French as yet unreformed. But Molière did not yield; he counter-attacked. After quoting a well-known sonnet in *The Misanthrope*, he gives what amounts to his *ars poetica:*

> Ce style figuré dont on fait vanité,
> Sort du bon caractère et de la vérité;
> Ce n'est que jeu de mots, qu'affectation pure,
> Et ce n'est point ainsi que parle la nature,
> Le méchant goût du siècle en cela me fait peur; . . .

and this dissenter recites for contrast a popular song of the previous age.

It does not follow from this creed that Molière is all simplicity and bluff common sense. In the course of his long, quite Shavian discussions, he hits off human traits in words of the greatest subtlety—and rapidity. His lines deserve the same kind of analysis that has been given to Racine's. They would show, too, that unlike the tragic poet, Molière had ideas about the regime. In the Prologue of *Amphitryon* again, he has Mercury complain of Jupiter, who "at the top of the sky" is always "corseted stiff" and "imprisoned in his grandeur." Louis XIV did not seem to mind—or to perceive—and it is to his credit that he defended the poet against the repeated cabals of his rivals and detractors.

The same combination of qualities and liberties as in Molière marks the work of La Fontaine, though in a tone and manner altogether different. For one thing, the *vers libre* is the medium throughout his *Fables*, as the eight-syllable narrative line is that of his *Contes*. This *vers libre* includes the alexandrine as needed; it is reserved for moments of explanatory asides or grave reflection. The fables depend for their brevity on dramatic dialogue and spare narrative. In this La Fontaine differs from Clément Marot, who flourished before

---

This figured style of which the users are so proud / Is out of character and leaves truth behind. / It is but play with words and sheer affectation. / It is not the way Nature speaks. / This wretched taste of our time frightens me. (I, 2)

The sonnet, by the way, which Molière ascribes in the play to Oronte, was by Benserade, who thereafter never again claimed its authorship.

the Pléïade and who perfected a conversational style in poetry from which La Fontaine learned much. Art in La Fontaine is concentration. He creates the single central scene of what might be a play, and his power comes from vividness and surprise delivered in what seems the most obvious words.

To gauge how far those words are from casual and appreciate the concealed art of their naturalness, one should read more than the few fables that familiarity has turned into clichés like Shakespearean tags. And yet such a well-known one as that about the oak and the reed ends with a picture that no repetition can dim:

> . . . Comme il disait ces mots,
> Du bout de l'horizon accourt avec furie
> Le plus terrible des enfants
> Que le Nord eût portés jusque là dans ses flancs.
> L'arbre tient bon; le roseau plie.
> Le vent redouble ses efforts,
> Et fait si bien qu'il déracine
> Celui de qui la tête au ciel était voisine,
> Et dont les pieds touchaient à l'empire des morts.

If Horace was a poet, La Fontaine must be held one too. And certainly, the modern "demotic" style of William Carlos Williams, Philip Larkin, or Marianne Moore can prepare readers for La Fontaine. It is only a pity that Miss Moore's attempt to translate him should be lacking in vivacity and exactitude.°

In the *Contes*, which are little known because for so long reputed obscene, La Fontaine retold in verse some medieval tales and others based on Boccaccio's or Bandello's. The surprising thing is that in spite of their outwardly joyful sensuality, there is—as in the *Fables*—an undertone of brooding close to pessimism. La Fontaine himself defines it as

> . . . (le) sombre plaisir d'un coeur mélancolique

As he was speaking, / From the horizon comes with a furious rush / The most fearful offspring / That the North ever carried in its womb. / The tree holds fast; the reed bends. / The wind redoubles its attack / And with such success that it uproots / Him whose head was neighbor to the skies / And whose feet reached into the kingdom of the dead. ("Le chêne et le roseau," *Fables*, I, 22)

. . . the somber delight of a melancholy heart. (*Les Amours de Psyché*, II)

No comparable mood is to be found in Boileau, though he too was unhappy. But his grievance was against the stupid and the vain, his strongest emotion being the critical. He worked hard at his rimes (as we heard him say to Molière) so as to perfect some vehement satires and the "Art of Poetry" that became only too influential. His odes and other praises of Louis XIV were written, one supposes, in cold blood—too cold to deserve anything other than Landor's vicious attack. But Boileau's mock epic *Le Lutrin* is a masterpiece.

It tells the quarrel between two clerical dignitaries over the removal of a writing desk in their church. Every line of the first five cantos is minted gold. The sixth and last, which moralizes about Justice, may not suit modern taste, but it is easy to omit—or to admire for its sheer power of elaboration: the long sermon on an obvious text is poetry as brilliant as what precedes.

Having quoted some lines from *Le Lutrin*—the opening scene that shows the canon's sleeping quarters—I yield to the temptation of adding his portrait:

> La jeunesse en sa fleur brille sur son visage:
> Son menton sur son sein descend à double étage,
> Et son corps, ramassé dans sa courte grosseur,
> Fait gémir les coussins sous sa molle épaisseur.

It is only fair to Boileau's memory to add that he was critical of himself in the same degree that he was of others. Early and late in life he bewailed the desperate toil needed to carry out his own commandments; in the Satire in which he begs Molière to teach him how to rime, he concludes:

> Ou, puisque tes soins y seraient superflus,
> Molière enseigne-moi l'art de ne rimer plus.

One of Boileau's targets, whom he shot at more than once—unjustly—was Philippe Quinault, whose tragedies are indeed inferior,

---

The bloom of youth glows on his countenance, / His chin rests in double tier upon his breast, / And his body, hunched into a short corpulence, / Makes the pillows groan beneath his flabby plumpness.

Or rather, since your efforts would be all in vain / Teach me, Molière, how not to rime again. (*Satire II*)

but whose comedies have merit and whose librettos for Lulli's operas are splendid. Here was another art of riming, which of course did not and could not conform to the rules if it was to fit musical form:

> Un son harmonieux se mêle au bruit des eaux;
> Les oiseaux enchantés se taisent pour l'entendre.
> Des charmes du sommeil j'ai peine à me défendre:
> Ce gazon, cet ombrage frais,
> Tout m'invite au repos.

Quinault would be accounted the equal of Metastasio and Da Ponte if the modern repertory included the seventeenth-century *Alceste, Armide, Persée* and other operas from his fertile pen. Most of these works dealt, like their kind, with love and violence. Quinault's special virtue was to write love lyrics that were tender without sentimentality and warlike verse without bombast. Voltaire was wrong to say: "Quinault was in his own art much superior to Lulli; he will always be read, whereas Lulli can no longer be sung."° But the intention of the judgment on Quinault was correct.

What the seventeenth-century can boast, then, is a Pléïade minus one: Corneille, Racine, Molière, La Fontaine, Boileau, and Quinault. And what their work shows is that the discipline imposed after the exuberance of the previous Pléïade neither fettered inspiration nor eliminated the freedoms that poets take no matter what system is in vogue. At the beginning of the period, it did look as if quasi police-state conditions would be enforced: Cardinal Richelieu, himself wanting an author's fame, put pressure on the newly formed Academy to censure Corneille's *Cid* for its violation of the three unities and other misdemeanors. The Academy complied—cautiously. Corneille defended himself, but thereafter observed the rules—grudgingly. From then on it was the public that judged—erratically.

For at any time, the public and, even more the critics, like to have a system, a yardstick, in fact a stick with which to cudgel the authors whose works they dislike for good or bad reasons. The Neo-classical system served that purpose pre-eminently and longer than most. It lasted from 1640 until 1830, when the staging of Hugo's *Hernani*

Harmonious sounds mingle with the noise of waters;/The birds, spellbound, keep silent so as to listen./The pleasures of slumber I can hardly resist:/This grassy spot, this cool shade/All tempts me to sleep. (*Armide*, Act II, sc. 3) caused an almost physical battle in the audience, and "the system" was no more.

That the French poets' testing ground during that span was the theatre is important and not hard to explain. The strength of Louis XIV's regime lay in its control over the nobility, which had threatened centralized monarchy for one hundred fifty years. Control was exercised through compulsory attendance at court, which kept (as it were) private life public. Ceremonial was serious business, and relief from it through entertainment also had political value. The theatre supplied the one and reinforced the other by depicting the imagined life of ancient courts, Greek and Roman. The narrow Neo-classical rules had a wider significance than the restraining of Pegasus.

What the tragic drama imposed on poetry was the stiffness and pomp that at first sight conceal from us moderns its passion. We forget that every line was accompanied by gesture, and that although the scenery was spare, the costumes were elaborate, extravagant— fantastic hats matching dresses that can only be called architectural; nothing like our idea of "classic simplicity," nor anything that could be worn off the boards.

Another antidote, surcease from etiquette and matters of state, was comedy, the medium Molière seized on to undermine all these pretensions: the bourgeois gentilhomme is disarming and lovable in his naturalness, and ridiculous only in his efforts to live up to the great. Molière alone managed by his poetic genius to keep the language of comedy from being perverted by the tragic muse. La Fontaine, the first of Bohemians, did the same by ignoring the existence of the court. Once, when he went there to present his book to the King, he forgot the book; returning with the purse graciously given, he mislaid the purse. But the *Fables* accurately show the courtier, the charlatan, the intriguer—and the monarch, both in his magnanimous and his misguided stance.

In sum, the great poets of seventeenth-century France in their several ways practiced social criticism. On two occasions the lesson deeply shocked the public: Racine's *Phèdre* showed sexual passion so vividly as to discompose habitués of elegant adultery; the play was fiercely attacked and Racine gave up writing for the public stage. On his side, Molière's *Tartuffe* showed up the seeming devout with such vigor that the growing party of puritans at court nearly succeeded in destroying the author. As in the play itself, he was saved by the king's intervention; but at Molière's death his enemies created a near-riot to prevent his burial in consecrated ground. The politics of poetry form no part of its artistic merit; they must nevertheless be understood, because they affect the poet's attitudes and limit or extend his opportunities. What is due to unavoidable coercion must not be imputed to free choice.

Natural curiosity at this point suggests the question why the facts so far presented have not been made familiar to every reader of English poetry who has ventured into French. I am sometimes tempted to think that even readers of French interested in the Neoclassic period still see it through the eyes of those who call it *le grand siècle*, see it, that is, as calm, unified, self-controlled and sublime, rather than as a battlefield of ideas, where the dissidents were in peril, they being the ones we now admire as if they represented the establishment.

Again, for English readers, why has there been no classic exposition of the forms and rules, their application and raison d'être?° True, one "defense" was made in 1912 by Emile Legouis, an esteemed student of English literature.° His essay was concerned like mine with the English critics and it answered them with moderate fervor supported by a few examples. It did not go into the labyrinth of rules and reasons, nor give a systematic account of poets and periods. Its chief contribution was to show the great influence of thirteenth-century French literature and its invigoration of English poetry by imparting to it *clarté*. By this Legouis meant not lucid expression, but the sunlit view of existence found, say, in Chaucer, which replaced the gloom of his Anglo-Saxon predecessors.

Shortly before Legouis, John C. Bailey published *The Claims of French Poetry*, in which he discussed French drama and seven poets from Marot to Heredia. Chapters point out qualities fairly enough and encourage appreciation by quotation and comment. By the end, one is sure that French poetry can make genuine claims; but they are denied the highest rating. Comparisons with Greek, German, and English poets (plus Dante) leave France without any truly great poetry. It is just very fine.

Henry Francis Cary, in the mid-nineteenth century, had done a more perceptive survey.° *The Early French Poets* is brilliant and subtle; but then he was the translator of Dante and he knew as a scholar *and* a poet the four centuries that embrace his two dozen subjects. Unfortunately his essays accompanied by examples have long been out of print.

In recent years at least three scholarly books have dealt at length with French verse; their titles will be found in the Notes.° But they do nothing to meet the case head on. One book discusses very ably the merits of French poetry—esthetic cause and effect in the work of the last two hundred years. Another supplies "background," but only of modern poetry; and the third, again, confines "appreciation" to the moderns. A reader who wants to understand the peculiarities of French poetics, which means seeing the role of language and of history in the making of the rules and forms, receives no help. He would learn more from a much older work, George Marsh's superb *Lectures on the English Language*, in which chapters 23 to 25 take up rime and its conditions in the Continental languages as compared with the English.°

The more recent books, moreover, leave the old impression that French poetry begins late. If an inquiring mind wants to look into the dark backward and abysm of time, what is he to do? Just a few days ago, a friend of mine asked, "What about Voltaire? Was he a great poet?—Was he a poet at all?" The questioner has an excellent reading knowledge of French and speaks the language efficiently, but has no clue to the mysteries of French versification, let alone to the poetic resources of the language. I know of no work to which to refer him. He will have to wait until this essay is published.

V

No doubt you will say: "Everybody writes poetry."
My reply to that is: "*Nobody* is writing poetry."
—Diderot, *Lettre sur les sourds et muets* (1751)

Before screening Voltaire, we must take a look at Fénelon—not as a poet but as an astute critic of the extant rules of the game and indeed of the whole development of speech and thought since Ronsard. In 1714, just one year before the death of Louis XIV, Fénelon, archbishop of Cambrai, indited a *Letter to the Academy* that was published shortly after his own death, the same year as the king. It is a detailed answer to a general request for advice that the Academy addressed to its members as to grammar, rhetoric, and lexicography.

All these subjects Fénelon treats in the light of a moral conviction he had come to early in life, and he did not mince words in expressing it: "People in this country are so afraid of being 'low' that when they come to express their thoughts they usually sound flat and dry. We are held back by a false politeness, like provincials who want to be always clever and lofty and exquisite. They are perpetually stiff and would think it beneath them to call things by their right names."° In keeping with this view, Fénelon blames the purge that reduced the French vocabulary, which used to be "simple, direct, unafraid, lively, and passionate."°

It was wise to publish this document after the demise of the Sun King and his flatterers, for in effect it was calling them pompous snobs. The Regency after Louis was, by a natural reaction, a time of self-indulgence, and Fénelon was chiming in with the growing desire for relaxed behavior. With Fénelon, it was an esthetic principle: the rigid versification was enfeebling. "In trying to give their thoughts delicacy, [poets] make it difficult to follow their meaning. They strain the sense to catch the rime. . . . Rime makes our verses lose variety, ease, and harmony. Often the poet goes far afield to find one, and so adds length to his utterance; he needs two or three filler lines in order to write the one he really wants."°

Fénelon does not propose doing without rime, but he confesses to being bored by the regular alternation of paired masculines and feminines. "Irregular verses . . . with their unequal lengths and lack of system, give freedom to vary the measure and the cadence to suit the need for elevation or simplicity." He praises La Fontaine and Molière for using this emancipated "vers libre" and recommends natural diction for tragedy as well as comedy.°

This first great assault on "the system" did not destroy it. The habits of the public (and the actors) were too strong. Besides, writers of small talent always constitute a vested interest behind any well-established scheme that enables them to turn out an acceptable product. Yet though the eighteenth century kept on imitating (as they thought) the ancients in the shape of Neo-classic models, weariness set in and objections multiplied. Voltaire was too keen a critic not to see that dramatic poetry in France was in decline, but he could not make up his mind about the cause or causes. He tried to refurbish tragedy by turning to exotic subjects (*Mohammed*) or incidents from French history (*Du Guesclin*), while he also found fault at times with the language at his disposal and the eternal recurrence of the mute *e*. At other times, he thought that this same toneless vowel was the source of harmony in verse—and he was right both times. He just missed seeing the reason for the contradictory impressions.

On the language question, Diderot, not a poet but an uninhibited genius in prose, agreed with Fénelon a generation after him; and toward the very end of the period, Rivarol, the author of an essay on the language that quickly became famous (it was again an answer to a public inquiry by the Academy), gave in it a kind of summary of public opinion in the 1780s. Says Rivarol: "The imagination of the poet is hampered by the over-cautious genius of the language. The metaphors of foreign poets always go one degree higher than ours; they cling more closely to the figurative style and their poetry is more highly colored. It is generally true that oriental images are wild, Greek and Latin daring, and ours simply *justes*."°

This description of the current state of poetry right after the death of Voltaire was itself *juste*. But note the assumption that "the language" was inherently and incurably confined within the current limits. Rivarol dimly perceives another possibility: "Our great masters did not fail to conceal beneath the web of a clear and sober style some daring inventions. . . . and our language would indeed be in the lowest rank if the bulk of our good writers had not raised it to the highest by going against its nature (*en forçant son naturel*)."°

The future was to show what its nature could really be. Meanwhile the eighteenth century witnessed no master hand to "force the language" as Rivarol expected a poet to do. Writers continued to use verse for tragedy on the old pattern. The only innovation was in the subjects. Crébillon took Aristotle literally about pity and terror and delivered shocks and horrors such as had been forbidden earlier—in short, wrote melodrama. His *Atrée et Thyeste*, which Poe liked to quote from, was a great success. Voltaire used new material as we saw. For other escapes from routine, authors including Voltaire cultivated the didactic poem, the epistle, the ode, and the lighter genres, especially the epigram.

In all these, the rime scheme, length of line, and shape of stanza offered free choices. Excellent work was done in these forms, though none of it can qualify as great poetry. Still, Voltaire's versified argument on the fearful Lisbon earthquake of 1755, his praise of his own enlightened time in *Le Mondain*, and his satirical pieces for innumerable occasions show consummate versifying skill and make very good reading.° Here is a short sample, the subject being the ancient Greek poet Pindar:

> Sors du tombeau, divin Pindare,
> Toi qui célébras autrefois
> Les chevaux de quelques bourgeois

> Ou de Corinthe ou de Mégare;
> Toi qui possédas le talent
> De parler beaucoup sans rien dire;
> Toi qui modulas savamment
> Des vers que personne n'entend,
> Et qu'il faut toujours qu'on admire.

By specializing in the ode, Jean-Baptiste Rousseau acquired in his day the reputation of a great lyricist. He was only an accomplished versifier of panegyrics and religious themes. He summed up his century's journeyman view of the art when he said that one learns to make verses the way one learns to play chess.* A more gifted writer named Gresset devoted himself to what goes by the name of *badinage*, of which one specimen won him instant fame. It still charms by its humor and its perfect handling of tone and form. It is a small mock-epic entitled *Vert-Vert* after its hero who—or which—is a parrot. The bird has been nicely brought up, in a convent, where he is an object of love and wonder. He goes on his travels and sees the world, only to come back corrupted in language and disillusioned in spirit. While he was still unspoiled and well-loved by the sisters, he was the life of the party:

> Il n'était point d'agréable partie
> S'il n'y venait briller, caracoler,
> Papilloner, siffler, rossignoler;
> Il badinait, mais avec modestie,
> Avec cet air timide et tout prudent
> Qu'une novice a même en badinant.

Arise from your grave, divine Pindar, / You who in the past extolled / The horses of several bourgeois / From Corinth or Megara; / You who had the talent / Of speaking much without saying aught, / You who skilfully warbled verses / That nobody now can understand / But is expected to admire. (Ode XVII: "Galimatias Pindarique," 1766 or 1768)

No party was any fun / Unless he was there to shine and bustle about, / Flit like a butterfly, whistle, and ape the nightingale. / He fooled around, but quite modestly / Looking timid, acting prudent / Just as a novice sister acts while fooling. (*Vert-Vert*, I)

---

* It is but fair to add that one excellent French critic, André Thérive, finds at least three great lyricists in the eighteenth century—Lefranc de Pompignan, Ecouchard-Lebrun, and J.-B. Rousseau—and two very fine ones: Léonard Thomas and Nicolas Gilbert. (*Le Retour d'Amazan*, Paris, 1926, p. 316)

The rime scheme is free and a small point to note is the trio of verbs in the third line, which only the light genre could tolerate.

These several deviations in genre, form, diction, and subject-matter were signs of restlessness. As in England, though more faintly, writers and public in eighteenth-century France wanted something new and did not know where to find it. Some attempt was made to acclimate Shakespeare through translation, for in England he was beginning to make a comeback after one hundred fifty years of mingled scorn and condescension. But his French translators, in trying to make him acceptable, unavoidably denatured his genius. He was neither his English self nor a good French one.

Besides, Voltaire in old age wrote a Letter to the Academy (the post-office of literature) against Shakespeare as the threat to civilized entertainment. Voltaire could read him in the original and had in fact appropriated passages from him for his own play on Julius Caesar; but the few gleams he could discern of Shakespearean poetry were, he said, obscured by the dark fumes of a savage, untutored mind: Crébillon made his actors describe horrible deeds; Shakespeare showed them. No doubt French tragedy had become monotonous; but Shakespeare enlivened his in unforgivable ways—by comic scenes and prose dialogue spoken by characters of low degree. This detestable mixture was the negation of art.

Though the year was 1776, this diatribe was clearly not a declaration of independence from the reigning system. Given the critiques and the boredom, the end of the century ought to have seen its withering away; but no, the Abbé Delille, the translator of *Paradise Lost* and Landor's chosen victim, was still turning out flaccid alexandrines obedient to all the rules. His mastery consisted in devising splendid circumlocutions to avoid naming vulgar things:

> Là, le sable dissous par les feux dévorants
> Pour les palais des rois brille en murs transparents.

This couplet stands for *glass-making shop*.

England was enduring the same sort of genteel versification but at least a few genuine poets had emerged who sang a somewhat new tune—Gray, Collins, Warton, Akenside. Still, that newness was not

---

There, devouring fires are dissolving sand / To make transparent walls for the palaces of kings. (*Les Trois règnes*)

conspicuous: as late as 1783, Blake in an address "To the Muses" wonders whether they have "forsaken poetry," because

> The languid strings do scarcely move,
> The sound is forced, the notes are few!

It took the advent of two geniuses, one in England, one in France, before these countries shed the Neo-classic uniform altogether and began once again to make great poetry. More, the emancipation inaugurated a new conception of the art itself, and of the poet as well; both innovations arising from new feelings about life, and in the process changing the character of the literary language.

> 'Tis not enough no harshness gives offence,
> The sound must seem an Echo to the sense.
> —Pope, *An Essay on Criticism* (1711)

Since the medium of poetry is language, it is not surprising that in shrinking the vocabulary and enforcing canons of propriety, the Neo-classic ideal should have made poetry the reverse of exuberant and colorful. This linguistic puritanism was justified in its own eyes by the sincere belief that it served the progression from a rude, barbarous age—the sixteenth century—to the present polite and civilized seventeenth and eighteenth. But poets could not wholly divest themselves of the feeling for words and, as I said in passing, even at the peak of self-restraint there was talk of harmony and poets were judged in part by their success in achieving it.

The term harmony is anything but clear or easy to define. And when one comes to compare periods on the point, the subject begins to appear in all its complexity. The evolution from Dryden to Swinburne, from Malherbe to Victor Hugo is no linear increase in harmonic skill or interest; it is a radical change of purpose and the exploiting of different resources in different historical phases of the language. I think I see in the poetics of the two countries since the Renaissance three different forms of the quality called the harmony of verse. Each is rooted in distinct properties of human speech, and taken together, all present a psychological puzzle that eludes definition almost as much as solution. Here, poised chronologically between Voltaire and Victor Hugo, is the place to consider the facts and offer surmises.

First, although poets are spoken of as having or not having a good ear, the evidence is that verse harmony has nothing to do with any musical gift except the sense of rhythm. Even that is a weak connection, because verbal rhythm obeys no strict measure. True, as noted earlier, the Renaissance poets were fascinated by the longs and shorts of ancient Greek and Latin meters, and both in England and in France attempts were made to imitate them with modern words. But the ventures failed precisely because in these words there are no longs and shorts of the true kind.

What followed was the striving for comparable harmony through fluidity of phrase, smoothness, and variety without shock. These allowed the composer of music to set the verse agreeably, and the ear was pleased in reading or recitation when poetry began to do without notes. It must indeed be sayable, particularly if intended for the stage. This quality, which sufficed for a good while, might be called negative harmony; it was the fruit of avoidance. It reminds one of Chopin's habitual way of passing judgment on a piece of music: *Je ne vois rien qui me choque.*

In the French poetry of the seventeenth century, it was often (French being a vowel language) the too close repetiton of the same vowel that "shocked." Malherbe criticized a fellow poet sharply for writing *comparable à ma flamme;* he highlighted the error by writing it: *parablamafla,* which to a French ear makes it stand out as not only ugly but ridiculous. The same effect can result from mismanaging consonants. Voltaire was deft, but he stumbled badly when he wrote

Non, il n'est rien que Nanine n'honore

Read straight through as it should be, this comes out as *Naneenuhnunnor* and is absurd.

I find in it nothing that shocks me.

No: there is nothing that Nanine does not grace. (*Nanine ou le préjugé vaincu,* III, 8)

There are permanent obstacles to sweet sound in the language itself—in any language. In French, the worst are the many connectives that contain *qu*. It is bad enough to have to say *quelque*, it would ruin harmony to write *quelque accident* (= kelkaks). Likewise with the harsh consonant *t* and its cognate *d*, which may lurk unheard till activated by liaison: *tarde à t'attendre* (= *tardatat*). Add to these the desirability of keeping similar verb forms from recurring close together and the exclusion of rimes based on an identical suffix (*patiemment / ardemment*), and it is clear how incessant the work of ensuring negative harmony was for the poet whom today we may suppose to have been indifferent to sounds.

The second degree of harmonic interest is the curious one most compactly stated by Pope in the couplet at the head of this section. It records an ancient principle, and I call it curious because it seems a platitude and yet is hard to understand, or at least to explain. How can sound echo sense? Pope is ready with examples:

> Soft is the strain when Zephyr gently blows,
> And the smooth stream in smoother numbers flows;
> But when loud surges lash the sounding shore,
> The hoarse rough verse should like the torrent roar.

This demand for echo is plausible for the events he chose to illustrate, though it involves a kind of tautology; but how is echoing managed where no events take place, in verse that discourses on noiseless matters?

Two notions, as I think, are confused in Pope's mind: once the polishing away of "offence" has been done, there is the goal of choosing words that are most apt for the idea—the words that make the reader rejoice while he vaguely thinks of those other "words not used" I referred to on an earlier page. This sense of perfect fitness, this "felicity of phrase," which combines the natural with the unusual or strange, produces such a pleasure that we *imagine* the sound and rhythm of the words echo the sense. They merely supply it attractively.

That is one of the two harmonies I believe to be confused. The other is found in Pope's examples, where the words seem to add to the sense, to decorate it with color and energy. Critical theory is not at all clear about the source of the effect. Why do "soft" and "smooth" sound soft and smooth? Or do they? The uncertainty is hastily covered up by the Greek word onomatopoeia—"to make by naming." To readers who like poetry so much that they also read essays about poets, nothing is so familiar as a passage in which the writer, having quoted a few lines that he admires, goes on to explain by onomatopoeia why they are admirable. "Notice," he will say, "the alternation of *l* and *r*, repeated in the second line, and rhythmically punctuated there by the strong *d* and *k* sounds, which convey the conflict between indolence and duty which is the theme of the stanza."

I do not believe a word of it. Onomatopoeia is a fiction. I discovered its illusory character when many years ago a Japanese friend with whom I often discussed literature told me that to him and some of his English-speaking friends the most beautiful word in our language was "cellardoor." It was not beautiful to me and I wondered where its evocative power lay for the Japanese. Was it because they find *l* and *r* difficult to pronounce, and the word thus acquires remoteness and enchantment? I asked, and learned also that Tatsuo Sakuma, my friend, had never seen an American cellar door, either inside a house or outside—the usual two flaps on a sloping ledge. No doubt that lack of visual familiarity added to the word's appeal. I concluded that its charmlessness to speakers of English lay simply in its meaning. It has the *l* and *r* sounds and *d* and long *o* dear to the analysts of verse music, but it is prosaic. Compare with it "celandine," where the image of the flower at once makes the sound lovely.

The magic, color, music of the words said to be onomatopoetic in poetry is due primarily to their meaning. Take some of Pope's own choices. "Soft is the strain" sounds gentle indeed, because of what it says. But "Tough is the strain," with virtually the same sounds, conveys the opposite of ease and gentleness. Indeed, the word "strain" is enough by itself to make my point: supply the right context and it will "echo" groaning effort as readily as airy music. And in Pope's last two lines, the arrangements of *l*'s, *r*'s, and *s*'s is exactly that which elsewhere would be pointed to as making mellifluous music. "Roar" is not in itself a loud word; it is much less so than "bore." Only at the halting "*hoarse* rough verse" does diction add anything to the sense—and it is rhythm that does it, not melody.

Doubts may persist on this issue when one thinks of a special class of words that I shall take up later. Here I want to return to the French poets and illustrate a further fallacy. In an excellent book on Baudelaire's versification, Albert Cassagne compares two versions of a stanza in *Jet d'Eau*. It is, the critic tells us, "a mixture of the most intense sensuousness with melancholy, and in the rimes as well as in the body of the verses, the high clear notes alternate with the low somber ones according to the character of the emotion:"°

> La gerbe d'eau qui verse
> Ses mille fleurs
> Que la lune traverse
> De ses lueurs
> Tombe comme une averse ·
> De larges pleurs.

This was the poet's first version. "He reflected that the desired effect of contrast between the sad and the cheerful was not sufficiently marked by the opposite tones of the clear vowel *e* and the low-pitched *eu*. So he recast the refrain and replaced the clear vowel with a higher and sharper one:

> La gerbe épanouie
> En mille fleurs
> Où Phébé réjouie
> Mets ses couleurs
> Tombe comme une pluie
> De larges pleurs

The critic has assumed that *i* contrasts more strongly with *eu*— which I think is true; that therefore it indicates a sort of distance between them; and that this distance suggests the oposition between gaiety and sorrow. Perhaps so; poetry is open to varied interpretations. But this one proves too much: if Baudelaire did intend the contrast by means of the paired vowels, then his first four lines are a blunder, for the second and fourth end in the low (sad) *eu* while they describe gay "flowers" and "colors." The emotional contrast comes only in lines five and six. On the critic's theory, the *i-eu* relation should be there and nowhere else.

A more plausible reason for Baudelaire's revising is the dubious legitimacy, as well as the false implication and poor quality, of the first rime: *verse* and *averse* are really the same word rather than a rich

---

The spray that pours / A thousand flowers / Through which the moon / Throws its beams / Ends in a shower / Of big tears.

The spray outspread / In a thousand flowers / On which happy Phoebe / Casts its colors / Falls like a shower / Of big tears.

rime; *traverse* (= goes across) seems forced; and *averse* is too commonplace a word to introduce the lofty term *pleurs*. Last and most regrettable, a spray of water that pours down flowers is—shall we say?—an unexamined metaphor: the spray does not pour anything—it *is* the pouring. Baudelaire, on a second look, perceived the error and hit upon *épanouie*, which is a lovely word; it describes flowers when they are fully opened. In all this, no need of onomatopoeia to justify the rewriting.

A more recent critic, Maurice Grammont, in a massive study of *Le vers français*, devotes a third of it to harmony, of which he claims to have discovered the scientific law: the various types of vowel, he says, must succeed one another in a certain order. "That is the whole secret of harmony in French verse."° There follows an elaborate classification of the sounds and a schema for their harmonious succession. It is ingenious, it works in the examples chosen, it breaks down when carried farther and wider. It also neglects that important troublemaker for theorists—changes in pronunciation. I shall take that up when the issue of direct imitation—onomatopoeia—has been laid to rest.

The doubts about it that I mentioned above boil down to the question whether some words are not onomatopoetic by nature and origin—"splash," "crash," "croak," "murmur," "moan," "hiss," etc., with a smaller, even more rackety group made up of "miaow," "bow-wow," "ding-dong," and the like. The latter I leave out of account as being not properly words but imitations for nursery use rather than literature or conversation; though here again, effectiveness depends on meaning: no one thinks of a dog barking when one says or hears the word *Bauhaus*. Context is omnipotent.

Now let us test as it were in action the other, larger group of words. Tennyson is famous for their adroit employment; every believer in onomatopoeia quotes from *The Princess:*

> The moan of doves in immemorial elms
> And murmuring of innumerable bees

The recurrent *m*'s and *n*'s are supposed to copy the reality. But forget the words and fill your mind's ear with the moaning and the buzzing, for—come to think of it—do bees buzz or murmur? A little of both? They hum too, so that we have three different renderings for what in nature is one. And the sound in nature does not include the *r* of "murmur," the *h* of "hum," or the *b* of "buzz." The verbal imitation is certainly partial and impure.

Nor is this all. Go to another language. In French bees *bourdonnent*, with the intrusive *b* and *r* and a bunch of *n*'s—not an *m* in sight or in the ear. Turn to Tennyson's moaning of doves. What do the doves do in France? *Elles roucoulent*, a more liquid operation that seems to capture a clear *k* sound. Tennyson leaves out both liquidity and the catch in the throat. Returning to his "murmur" we may well ask whether the word as commonly used does not also fit the noise of an angry crowd; and again, the half-swallowed utterance of a person too shy to speak out.

I do not see what to conclude but that so-called onomatopoeia is the product of a convention by which a single element, more or less correctly chosen from a complex natural sound, stands for that complex and is then extended, with less and less accuracy, to other vaguely similar situations. In the end, it is the meaning attached to the word through variable uses which gives the impression that the word suggests in turn each of these quite different sounds. Usage, meaning does the work.

This roundabout effectiveness explains the diversity among languages as to what copies reality: English "splash" = French *gicler*, *éclabousser*; "croak" = *coasser*; and so on. Even the directly imitative attempts differ: English "cock-a-doodle-do" corresponds to *cocorico*—the sound *k* is the only common feature, as posited in the theory I offer. German, closer to English, does hardly better: frogs that croak in English *quaken* or *quäken* in German, and rooks that *caw* for us *krächzen* across the North Sea. These examples, moreover, are efforts at imitation nearest to parroting nature. The last of them makes one think of "crash," which it is all too easy to believe echoes the sound of breakage. But we use it for the fall of a glass on the floor and of a plane from the skies, as well as for the collision of two cars—three different sounds.

There is really no telling what will strike the would-be imitator as suggestive. A Chinese poet says that the wind goes *liao-liao*—surely not a wind from the West. With us it "soughs" (suffs) or whistles. But other things, not at all wind-like, also whistle. Thus Racine describes the appearance of the Furies during Orestes' hallucination:

> Pour qui sont ces serpents qui sifflent sur vos têtes?

Whom are these serpents for that whistle atop your heads? (*Andromaque*, V, 5)

This much-praised line states quite rightly that the serpents whistle. But onomatopoeia is supposedly achieved by means of the five *s*'s. Now, did the snakes hiss or whistle?

According to convention either will do; but it *is* a convention, and one that holds good only when the meaning gives it support. For in another admirable passage Racine has:

> Ariane, ma soeur, de quel amour blessée
> Vous mourûtes aux bords où vous fûtes laissée!

Here the succession of *s*'s has no zoological overtones, no hiss of hate. On the contrary, it helps to express the acme of tender solicitude. Letters and sounds seem infinitely malleable, and it is the pressure of meaning that changes their character, sometimes radically, In French, for example, *l'époux* (spouse) is in frequent use and always with the connotation of sweet fidelity. Its neighbor in sound *les poux*, as all know from Rimbaud's famous poem, means lice. But this does not in the least infect the other word.

A final example will show how several different languages spanning centuries of use have hit on the same sound to represent both identical *and opposite* impressions. Leconte de Lisle has a group of lines that skillfully evoke the visual and the auditory reality:

> Au tintement de l'eau dans les porphyres roux
> Les rosiers de l'Iran mêlent leurs frais murmures,
> Et les ramiers rêveurs leurs roucoulements doux.

Here we have enough *l*'s and *r*'s to please the lover of liquidity, but *tintement* (tinkling) is the word also used for church bells—not a watery sound. It reminds us of Poe's poem "The Bells," in which he uses "tintinnabulation" imitatively; it is the same word in another form. It implies a clanging, and so does the French *tintamarre*—a loud cacophonous noise, whether natural or caused by a human brawl. In English we call it more briefly a *din*. That is in fact the root of all four

---

Ariane, my sister, by what a cruel love you were stricken, / And died on those shores where you were abandoned! (*Phèdre*, I, 3)

With the water tinkling in the russet marble [basins], / The Persian rose bushes blend their cool murmurings / And the dreamy wood doves their soft cooings. ("La Vérandah," *Poèmes Barbares*)

words: the Sanskrit *dhun*, which means simply "sound," neither loud nor soft, pleasant nor unpleasant. Leconte's *tintement* (so close to *tintamarre*) is therefore lovely not by itself but by association with the scene. I might add that the *murmure* which pops up again in the next line is here rescued, so to speak, from Tennyson's humming bees, from the angry crowd, and the mumbling speaker, to suggest now a gentle breeze *soughing* through a rosebush.

With their stronger and more numerous consonants, the Germanic languages would seem to have a better opportunity to produce genuine onomatopoeias, because the sounds of nature have an edge that the vowels which govern French cannot approximate. That is as may be. But until further notice I shall believe that English can show only one true onomatopoeia, and that one not intended; it is the word *adenoidal*.

None of the foregoing means that verbal "music" is an illusion; anybody who reads poetry with pleasure knows that it exists; but beyond the negative harmony I discussed above, the source of that pleasure remains elusive, as the pursuit of echo and onomatopoeia has shown. And there is yet another difficulty to conjure with: even the negative smoothness has a factually shaky basis. Pronunciation changes over time and place, and the relations among sounds change with it. To put it another way, the sound of a line of poetry is not fixed; it is indefinitely variable.

Since judgments in these matters are existential—a verse's prosperity lying in the individual's ear—I may perhaps indulge in personal reminiscence. Leconte de Lisle's vignette first came into my ken when read aloud by my lycée professor; he extolled it as supreme art and repeated it with unction. He was a man from the South of France and trilled his *r*'s in a fashion that the class had got used to in prose but that struck us again as hilarious when they resounded in these particular lines—les *porr-phyrrres-rrr*oux: the vibrating tip of the tongue gave forth almost a *d*, as do some English voices in saying *very* (*vedy*). And when it came to *murmures*, the contrast between the fluted sound intended by the poet and the reciter's drum-like rendering had us fighting to keep straight faces and avoid punishment.

Obviously, to the reciter it was sublime music. What did he hear? The question is even more pertinently put to the poet, who may have heard the sounds current in Reunion Island, in the Indian Ocean, where he was born, or those he later acquired in Paris. Besides, he lived well before that lycée lecture took place, and French had changed in half a century. My great-grandmother, who was born in 1830 and took a particular interest in my education, had a poor opinion of the way my classmates and I pronounced the language. The pronoun *ils* with the *l* sounded, the word *papillon* ending in -*yon* instead of -*lion*, the city of *Bruxelles* as if *x* should be heard and not *ss*— these and other horrors made her shake her head.

Having been reared before the days of television and of hands-off parents, she spoke like the educated people of the generation before hers, namely that of the early 1800s. As a result, I learned from her how Lamartine and Musset ought to sound—which liaisons to make or omit, the values of *h*, the three different ways of handling double *l*, the duty of sounding two *m*'s in *immédiat* but only one in *immeuble*, and what final or median consonants to eliminate—*fils* pronounced *fi*, *assomption*, *assontion*, *monsieur* not with *muh* but with *mo*, and much else. It took some effort to please her and remember not to carry these reformed utterings back to school, where they would be reproved by the teachers and ridiculed by the fellows. But the experience taught me that the melody I thought I heard in a poem was to an unknown extent the effect of the pronunciation of my time.

The evidence about past ways of speaking is plentiful and adds to the puzzle about the pleasure for the senses we think embodied in poems of an earlier day. We know that from the Middle Ages down to the seventeenth century, French made war on consonants wherever found. Not only were all possible finals dropped (as *er* has become *é*), but internal *ct* was at one time reduced to *t* (*pacte* = patte), -*al* amounted to *au*, -*ol* to *ou*, and *quel* to *queu*. Nouns in -*eur* were spoken -*eu* (*porteur*, *chasseur* = *porteu*, *chasseu*).° In another fad, also of short duration, internal *r* was pronounced *s*; a relic of this vagary is embalmed in the common word *chaise*, originally *chaire* as in English "chair."

As a general rule of permanent application, two consonants together caused the suppression of the stronger. When Racine in the 1600s wrote *puisqu'il*, he said and heard *pui-qui*. To my ear and everybody else's from 1800 to the present, *pui-qui* is a silly sound. And it is disappointing to think that for Racine also the lovely word for swan—*cygne*, which owes its charm to the *gn* (pronounced like Spanish ñ)—was sounded simply *cine*: the name without the charm! Of course, many of these alterations were later reversed, just as the medieval license (also due to lax pronunciation) by which the nasal *in* rimed with plain *i* came to be abolished. Others of those variations may denature for us the very meanings intended, and since such changes have taken place in different generations and unevenly in the several provinces, there is no assurance that in reading Villon or Marot or Molière one is enjoying *their* harmony.

So much for the fiddling with consonants. The vowels have wobbled too. At one time, every *en* was *an*, not as now a capricious choice of *an* or *in*. Molière's servant parts, particularly in *Don Juan*, faithfully reproduce the old grammar and pronunciation that he observed in his provincial tours and that was formerly the speech of Francis I and his Court a hundred years before: *j'av*ONS BIAN *raison; tu vois* BIAN QU'I[ls] *nous appel*ONT.

One feature of this earlier French accounts for a peculiarity in spelling down to Voltaire and beyond. The diphthong *oi* in *roi, foi,* and the like is normally pronounced *wa*. At some point—perhaps after the influx of Italians with Catherine de Medici in the 1550s—the sound changed, first, to *wey: roi* came out as *rouet* and the verb forms in *oit, oient* as if spelled *avouet* and so on. Riming would link *fouet* (whip) with *donnoit*. Molière rimes *froide* with *possède*. Later, the *ai* (*è*) sound predominated and the present spelling slowly caught up; Voltaire urged the Academy to approve *avait* in place of *avoit*, by then identical to the ear. Not until 1835 did the Academy comply. From this evolution comes the disparity between the national name *français* and the personal name *François*.

In this welter of vocal choices, nobody can say "This poet's lines should be read thus-and-so." What would happen (in our mind's ear) to the clicking elegance of Pope's *Rape of the Lock* if we heard the poet and his friends talk of "takin' tay in chaney coops edged with goold and feelin' obleeged if a lawd would jine them"? Some words in a verse from the past may confidently be assigned a value other than the modern one, but not all. When contemporary observers wrote books to inform posterity that "This is how people pronounce this type of word," they usually wanted to lay down the law—and not everybody agreed. Class distinctions, age, region, education, mix habits and sounds. Which brings us to the last of the variables, the poet himself.

To speak in the first person again, I have heard a score of poets read their works, in either of the languages that I can hear critically. Not

---

For: *j'avais bien raison; tu vois bien qu'ils nous appellent.* (I was right: can't you see they're calling us?) It has nothing to do with verse, but is relevant to French-English linguistic relations, that at this same court a common form of greeting was *"Comment le faites vous?"*—our "How do you do?" word for word. Who borrowed from whom is not clear; the idea is obvious without borrowing, as is shown by the modern U.S. variant "How're you doing?"

one performer impressed me with his or her sense of harmony. The greater number were frequently unintelligible, without the result being beautiful music. The better enunciators were of two kinds— they chanted or they did their best to make verse sound like ordinary conversation.

One exception to this disappointing report is not truly an exception. The great actor Firmin Gémier revealed to my ear the special harmony of Molière's verse. He did this, not in the course of acting at the Comédie Française, where his effects were blurred by the noises the other players made, but in an impromptu recital at a private house, where he delivered excerpts that he particularly liked. I say recital and not reading, because it is often reading, eyes on paper, that kills the poet's chance to be understood and perhaps to achieve harmony.° Nor do I mean to imply that all actors do justice to verbal music. Dame Sibyl Thorndike reciting "Shall I compare thee to a summer's day" nasalized the entire sonnet into the likeness of a dirge and drove away, in the fear of more, the most eager member of the audience.

On reflection, these facts seem to me to warrant a paradoxical view of verse harmony, even of negative harmony, since the smoothness we perceive can disappear when we substitute the strange sounds that were in use two, three, five centuries ago. Yet the belief in harmony has always existed; it inspired Aristophanes to pit Aeschylus against Euripides as the superior in that respect—it is a self-validating belief. A final anecdote is clinching. When Evgeny Yevtushenko was made an honorary member of the American Academy of Arts and Letters, I was seated next to him at lunch and we talked, in a mixture of French and English. The subject was mainly poetry and, toward the end, French poetry. Suddenly, the poet threw his head back and with a rapt expression began to declaim some lines. For a minute or two I could make out no word known to me. Then, by good luck I caught some syllables and by rapid induction decided I was hearing Verlaine's *Il pleure dans mon coeur comme il pleut sur la ville*.

Unquestionably, this charming ditty had conveyed its music to Yevtushenko: hearing it in his mind's ear, he reproduced it there— only there, for to me his rendering was cacophonous since I could make out no words: verbal music must be intelligible or it ceases to be verbal.

This series of puzzles forces me to accept a proposition that contains its own denial: certain verses generate sensuous harmony with-

---

In my heart is weeping like the rain in the town. (*Romances sans paroles*, III)

out affording any uniform sensory experience. When pronunciation changes in the history of a language, or by individual vagaries, the relation among the sounds appears to change also in some compensating way, doubtless influenced by meaning. A foreigner's distortion goes with his general distorted hearing of the language, modified by his understanding of it; and when the native poet in reading his own work dims his own music, it still rings as clear in his mind as when he composed it.

Meter is less volatile and rarely needs to be searched for; it discloses itself, sometimes unpleasantly. It is notorious in English literature that novelists who get carried away by strong feeling fall into iambic pentameters that mar the rhythm of prose. The fault is perhaps still more frequent in French when the subject is itself poetic. Flaubert's novel *Salammbô* about ancient Carthage numbers in its descriptions a good many alexandrines. French critics in the supposedly tone-deaf seventeenth century cautioned against this fault. The friends of Pascal and teachers of Racine, who lived as solitaries at Port Royal, wrote a rhetoric in which it is said that the best length for concluding a prose period is either five or seven syllables and sometimes eight; that is, it must be more or less than half an alexandrine verse. Care must be taken, moreover, that if the first unit ends with a masculine word, the predicate or complement be a feminine, presumably to avoid the slightest likeness to a riming pair. Some of these considerations will recur when we come to that nineteenth-century genre, the prose poem.

By the end of the Neo-classic period, the poetry produced was not even tolerable verse but rather metered prose, seldom rising above commonplace ideas and threadbare diction. Images other than circumlocutions for propriety were either clichés or timid, stunted growths. Voltaire in editing Corneille had half regretted this effect of Reason: "Ours is not an age in which a poet can address his soul or his [strong right] arm." These things had to change if poetry were to be seen or heard again. Revolution in politics came in 1789 and helped bring on the revolution in poetry. Message and language were made new, and in language the new meant more than the mere abandonment of "noble" words and accepted images. A new conception of literature as a whole found expression in what is called Romanticism, and that conception is still dominant.

Not only did negative harmony become positive musicality, but color was added—vivid, striking, strange, abundant. The written word in every genre must give the reader the instant impression of reality; indeed, all the senses must be addressed and by the most direct route—in short, concreteness in place of abstraction. Epithets and descriptions that had aroused only vague notions of pleasure or pain—"a most agreeable countryside," "a beauty as fair as one could wish," "a banquet to delight the refined taste"—must now be replaced by explicit terms, giving clear, sharp details. As Blake said: "To Generalize is to be an Idiot. To Particularize is the Alone Distinction of Merit."°

It is interesting to note that in English poetry of the transition period, this new mode of speech for arousing the senses came through the unfamiliar, the primitive or calculated strangeness—the virtue that dispels boredom. Strangeness came in the simple diction of the Border Ballads and the Scottish dialect of Burns, the Gaelic windiness of Ossian, and the contrived archaisms of Chatterton. Why did a comparable influence not come to the aid of French poets from the ballads of their own country? There were plenty of them, and of high quality, but they violated every canon of versification and if imitated could only destroy, not revivify it. The people in their songs had gone straight to the right sound and rhythm, regardless of spelling or polite usage: *J'irai me plaindre au duc(que) de Bourgogne*—meter requires the added *que*, which is a mispronunciation. The well-known *Auprès de ma blonde* starts off: *Dans le jardin d'mon père*—mute *e*'s are expendable. And in Nerval's collection hiatus is got over by inserting a letter or omitting one: *J'ai-z-un coquin de frère, T'[u]en as menti.*° Such freedom was not admissible in poetry addressed to the lettered—not with the Academy and the shade of Boileau looking on. In France, therefore, the painful transition occurred in a different way, through the small but precious output of Chénier's poetry.

His work has, to begin with, a chronological peculiarity. Chénier did not live to see the new century, yet I said that in his own, France produced no true poetry. The fact is that except for a couple of topical pieces, his work first saw the light in 1819, a year ahead of the first truly Romanticist work, Lamartine's *Méditations Poétiques*.

To speculate whether Chénier would have developed into a Romanticist poet is like wondering whether Shelley might not have turned into a Tory Member of Parliament. Better worth thinking about is what Chénier accomplished that was symptomatic; transition is a vague term, and I have the impression that the standard accounts do not make sufficiently vivid what Chénier achieved.

He effected a noticeable change in poetic diction by substituting a fresh set of Greek myths for the tired Roman ones of the Neoclassics, and he dropped many of the perfunctory images—*appas*, *feux*, *chaînes*, *charmes*, and others akin to "feathered tribe" and "resplendent orb" in English. Greek was native to Chénier through his mother, who married the French Consul in Constantinople, where André was born. He reveled in the many ancient stories that previous poets had neglected; the names, places, and kinships seemed by themselves to inspire him, and it was this unused, unspoiled atmosphere that he had in mind when he wrote:

> Sur des pensers nouveaux, faisons des vers antiques

By that last word he meant antiquity, not old style; and these "new thoughts" or themes he listed and discussed in a poem called *L'Invention*, which is his *art poétique*. The burden of it is the urgent necessity to stop imitating the models; or rather, to act just like them by *not* imitating. He asks why the young poets should

> Dire et redire cent fois ce que nous avons lu.
> L'esclave imitateur naît et s'évanouit;
> La nuit vient, le corps reste et son ombre s'enfuit.
> Ce n'est qu'aux inventeurs que la vie est promise.

He is sure that "august Poetry" will find the people

> Applaudir à grands cris une beauté nouvelle.

So aware is he of the means on which novelty depends that he discusses the issue Rivarol had raised about the fitness of the French language and asserts that it can readily be

> Doux, rapide, abondant, magnifique, nerveux.

———

On novel themes make verses in the ancient mode.

Tell and re-tell a hundred times what we all have read. / The slavish imitator is born and vanishes; / Night comes, the body stays behind and the shade takes flight. / To inventors alone is life assured.

Giving loud applause to beauty new in form.

Tender, swift, abundant, splendid, sinewy. (This verse is itself "daring" in having four cesuras—or none, as the reader decides.)

If French is ever thought weak in coloring, cold in tone, and timid, it is only because latter-day poets have brought it to that state. The masters—he cites Boileau, Racine, Rousseau, Buffon, and Montesquieu—used it in a manner that shows its "fruitful colors." Any true writer inflamed by his own genius thinks in a "langage imprévu" (unforeseen), "imagines" his words, and his figures of speech come to birth simultaneously with his ideas. Here Chénier uses the pregnant phrase (itself a new idea) *ce besoin de créer*—this need to create. In fact, his choice and range of proper names are by themselves enough to give his verse a new coloring and harmony.

Chénier was of his own time in considering Nature "the immense source of truth." Among nature's truths for poetry he included those produced by the developing sciences. This suggestion has been called illusory; it is pointed out that the truly scientific chemistry of Chénier's fellow victim in the Terror, Lavoisier, has never inspired a good poem. True, but a whole metaphorical vocabulary has come from science. It passes unnoticed precisely because it was adaptable to both literary and common expression.

In the event, Chénier never attempted to celebrate the evolutionary biology and the astrophysics that he studied and recommended for poetic use. He was guillotined for his few political verses in his thirty-second year, two days before Robespierre, whose death ended the Terror and would have set the poet free. Chénier kept writing even in prison, not publishing but accumulating and revising odes, elegies, idylls, epistles, and fragments for the longer works he projected.

In the 80-odd pieces that he left the prevailing note is the elegiac. His soul was moved by the eternal subjects: the passage of time and fleetingness of love; youth and death; and also—something new in his day—the sufferings of poverty, oppression, and injustice. His political indignation gave fire to splendid (and suicidal) invective, and his pensive temperament went with a characteristic unsentimental tenderness:

> Elle a vécu, Myrto, la jeune Tarentine!
> Un vaisseau la portait aux bords de Camarine:
> Là, l'hymen, les chansons, les flûtes, lentement
> Devaient la reconduire au seuil de son amant.

Her life is over, the Tarentine maid's / A vessel was taking her to Camarina: / There the wedding songs, with flutes were slowly / To lead her to the threshold of her lover's house . . . /

. . . .
Helas! chez ton amant tu n'es point ramenée,
Tu n'as point revêtu ta robe d'hyménée,
L'or autour de tes bras n'a point serré de noeuds,
Les doux parfums n'ont point coulé sur tes cheveux.

These opening and closing lines of an early poem are a good example of Chénier's distinctive voice. They also show his penchant for breaking the rigidity of the alexandrine while appearing not to do so. The first line varies the rhythm by halving the forepart into four- and two-syllable portions. The third does even more to establish triple time, in keeping with the musical scene. As for the final quatrain, it moves gradually from the general to the concrete, at midpoint goes past it, and ends in impressionism by means of a slightly unreal image. The very last line might have been written in 1890, not 1790. The great change had begun.

VII

. . . Modern poetry comes out of that
whirlwind of Romanticism and takes on,
of course, a thousand aspects, but one man
alone sums it up, one in whom all tradi-
tions, all inventions fuse together: Victor Hugo.
    —Louis Aragon,
        Avez-vous lu Victor Hugo? (1952)

I had been making notes for this essay over a good many years before I began to sort them early in 1985 and, as a result, to reread the poems they referred to in cryptic indications of title and page. Suddenly, I realized that the year was the centenary of Victor Hugo's death. In 1885 he had been given a national funeral as one of the makers of the Third Republic; a hundred years later he was again being feted

---

Alas! You were not escorted to his door, / You did not put on the wedding gown, / The gold band did not encircle your arm, / Sweet perfumes were not poured upon your hair. (*La jeune Tarentine*)

officially. Abroad, little notice was taken, although *Les Misérables* was enjoying a long Anglo-American run as, of all things, a musical. These conjunctions bring to the fore the great live issues of Romanticism—ill-begotten name!—and Hugo's Janus-like reputation in France and England. For to critics everywhere—both the conventional and the competent—Hugo *is* Romanticism in French poetry. That summary judgment is tenable if suitably qualified, and to qualify it one must first see what happened to verse after Chénier, whom we left, dead and unknown, before his century ended.

His collected poems, which first appeared in 1819, quickly made their way: new editions came out in 1826 and 1833: he evidently satisfied a new taste. Confirmation is given by the success in 1820 of Lamartine's *Méditations Poétiques*, a work whose genesis shows the "transition" completed. This young poet had begun writing verse on light subjects in the approved eighteenth-century style—trifles, *badinage*. By dint of painful, protracted reworkings and by taking advice from friends, he achieved a voice of his own. It was immediately felt to have made a break with the past.

To begin with, the words themselves were unfamiliar in verse. In a piece on "God Immaterial," one finds:

> Tel que le nageur nu, qui plonge dans les ondes,
> Dépose au bord des mers ses vêtements immondes,
> Et changeant de nature en changeant d'élément,
> Retrempe sa vigueur dans le flot écumant, . . .

"Naked swimmer" and "filthy clothes" are not "noble" expressions; they even jar a little with *ondes* and *flot écumant*, which have the old ring of polite indirection. But soon after we run into "leather sandals" and "a narrow belt," which would have made Delille choke had he been alive—such crude details in a parable about the Godhead! The classic measure is not altered—so far; but it is in later pages of the volume, where poems are found with lines of eight syllables that rime in various patterns. The alexandrine is no longer in sole command of the serious subject.

In addition, entire pieces are devoted to the description of nature. Jean-Jacques Rousseau had single-handed established the idea that

---

As the naked swimmer who dives into the waves / Puts down on the shore his filthy clothes, / And changing his nature by change of element / Tempers his strength anew in the foaming flood, . . .

man's relation to nature and appreciation of it were fit topics for
literature; but no French poet since the sixteenth century had made
either the theme of a "meditation," as Lamartine does in *Le Vallon:*

> Là, deux ruisseaux cachés sous des ponts de verdure,
> Tracent en serpentant les contours du vallon;
> Ils mêlent un moment leur onde et leur murmure,
> Et non loin de la source ils se perdent sans nom.

These bare facts—the stream's hidden, nameless existence and dis-
appearance—occasion the now obvious reflection about human life
and human love; it was not obvious until the Romanticist poets made
it so.

Lamartine went only a short way toward freeing verse, exploit-
ing new subjects, and stretching language without compunction.
The total role was left for Hugo, and that is the sense in which he
is Romanticism incarnate. As a revolutionist in literature his per-
formance, coupled with the size of his output, match Ronsard's
three hundred years earlier, and exceed it in variety and influence.
Hugo did for poetry in France what Wordsworth did for it in Eng-
land.

Indeed, if a modern Plutarch were to write Parallel Lives, those
two poets would make a perfect pair. Both changed the course of
poetry by reforming diction and subject matter in a vast body of
work. Both were moved by the French Revolution into political
consciousness and a concern for the poor and humble. Both studied
nature to find in it an answer to religious doubt and moral question-
ing. Both viewed themselves as bards, that is, wise men, prophets in
the Biblical sense, destined to give lifelong guidance to their people.
Their unconcealed vanity derived from this conviction, and so did
their incessant production—recording, commenting daily on events,
on their search and discoveries within the soul (theirs and other
men's); noting chance encounters, visits to places, accidents of their
private life—telling all. Some poets had severally done some of these
things in verse before, but none had felt it a duty to encompass the
whole range of individual existence in unabashed personal utterance.

That is why it is wrong to compare their output with the selected
publishings of other poets. One should regard much of what they

---

Here two rivulets hidden under bridges of greenery / Mark in their
meandering the contour of the valley; / They mingle for a moment their
waters and their murmur, / And not far from their source vanish namelessly.

wrote as diary entries, which their work habits cast automatically
into verse. Note how both took pains to date their poems and give
the place where they were written: it is the practice of the self-histo-
rian, the diarist. Seeing it for what it is should change the way we
regard that portion of their *oeuvre* we think dull, inferior, or repe-
titious.

Hugo went beyond Wordsworth in a number of respects. He was a
passionate lover, an active politician and pamphleteer, a copious
novelist and playwright, a Surrealist draftsman, a tireless student
of history and mythology, a panegyrist of Napoleon, and a writer
of political satire unexampled since Tacitus. These are no doubt
the reasons why Sartre thought Hugo "possessed a kind of super-
human power" and was "unquestionably the sovereign of the whole
century."° That Hugo's populist doctrine coupled with his copious-
ness made him hateful to the poets who came after him is not
surprising, especially when one considers how the public school
curriculum turned into clichés some of the best lines of "the great
Republican."

For the present purpose the Hugo that matters is the reformer of
French versification and its unquestioned master. He published as
early as 1822, but it is in 1826, with *Odes et Ballades*, that the fun
begins. The preface is a manifesto like Wordsworth and Coleridge's
to *Lyrical Ballads* a quarter-century earlier, though there is no link of
influence between them. The Lake Poets were not known in France
till later.

Lamartine had left the alexandrine regular; Chénier had been
bolder and bent it here and there; Hugo systematically loosened it
along its entire length. With him, the cesura comes at any point and
the sense frequently runs past the end of the line into the next. In the
line itself, thirty-six possible combinations of "cuts" (pauses) can be
made, notably the three-times-four syllables, which effectively
erases the halving of the line. It becomes a new kind of *vers libre*. The
rhythm can thereby follow mood and meaning, while the frame
provided by the rime and, as needed, a judicious return to the old
regularity, create between them an effective counterpoint.

> On vit, on parle, on a le ciel et les nuages
> Sur la tête; on se plaît aux livres des vieux sages;
> On lit Virgile et Dante; on va joyeusement

One lives and speaks and sees the sky / Above one's head; one enjoys the
wise old books / One reads Virgil and Dante and joyfully takes a trip /

En voiture publique à quelque endroit charmant,
En riant aux éclats de l'auberge et du gîte;
Le regard d'une femme en passant vous agite;
. . . .
On se sent faible et fort, on est petit et grand
On est flot dans la foule, âme dans la tempête;
Tout vient et passe; on est en deuil, on est en fête;
On arrive, on recule, on lutte avec effort—
Puis, le vaste et profond silence de la mort!

This passage, though not among the highest reaches of the new poetics, is typical enough to illustrate Hugo's emancipated alexandrine. The pauses in the first line punctuate the thought, which continues unbroken through the opening three syllables of line two, leaving nine more for another extended idea. Next comes what seems a regular half-and-half division to provide a kind of rest—except for the surprise of the enjambment (run-over), which comes as a descriptive afterthought. Together with the next line—eighteen syllables in all—it supplies the cadence. The very last of the group, though linked by the rime *gîte*/*agite*, delivers a thought quite foreign to the preceding. The net effect is of something *built* from end to end as a section, not assembled in self-contained pairs of lines.

In the second group, the third line is characteristic of the 3/4 rhythm that provides what might be called a second type of regularity, since it makes an even division into four syllables. All the other "cuts," in groups of three, four, five, or one, are at the will of the poet and do not answer a set expectation; the emphasis falls where he chooses, as in the last line, at *Puis*, after which the eleven unstressed syllables connote the headlong march to extinction. That last line and also the second show the readiness with which French allows the poet to use a long series of unaccented syllables, a rhythm that can sound slow or fast, depending on the combination of meaning and sound.

It hardly needs pointing out that the vocabulary is completely free of restraints. *Voiture publique* tells it all in one phrase, justifying Hugo's boast that he had put the red cap of the Revolution on the old

---

In a public vehicle to some delightful place / Laughing uproariously at the quaint lodgings; / A woman's glance in passing by stirs you up /. . . . One feels strong and weak, big and small / One is like a drop in the crowd and a soul in the storm / Things come and go; One is now in mourning, now jollifying / One arrives, retreats, struggles mightily—/ And then, the huge, deep silence of death. (*Les Contemplations*, IV, 11)

dictionary of noble words.* This declaration of independence was plain enough to the stunned audience of *Hernani* in 1830, when they heard casual mention in verse of a staircase, a handkerchief, and other monstrous things.

But though the overthrow of convention was shocking, its purpose was not destruction or anarchy and its exploitation was not brash. Victor Hugo and his peers—Musset, Vigny, Nerval, Gautier—were artists and they showed by their use of the new freedom that poetry in French could encompass in impeccable forms a range of feeling, vision, and thought hitherto unimagined. And of the group, Hugo— as Aragon points out—was the encyclopedic creator. For once, a qualified English critic concurred or rather, anticipated the judgment. Swinburne, shortly before his own death, summed up the sixty-three years of Hugo's production, the 175,000 lines (not counting the plays) by calling Hugo: "one of the very greatest among poets and among men; unsurpassed in sublimity of spirit, in spontaneity of utterance, in variety of power, and in perfection of workmanship . . . master of all the simplest as of all the subtlest melodies or symphonies of song that ever found expression in a Border ballad or a Pythian ode."°

Anyone who wants to follow the work of the master's hand in a great poem that combines harmony, color, imagination, and compression in dazzling perfection, should turn to *"La Fête chez Thérèse"* in *Les Contemplations*—eighty-eight lines of effortless virtuosity. In that poem, the rimes play the role that Sainte-Beuve and Banville assigned to them—to give unity and cadence. Because the flexible alexandrine defies expectation, its riming must be "rich." Merely sufficient rimes would feel like little more than assonance and so would not adequately mark the meter against which the free rhythmic pattern is to be perceived. In fertility and variety of rime, Hugo is unsurpassed and unsurpassable. By dint of reading in many fields, he acquired an immense vocabulary of common and proper nouns and used them with astonishing aptness and force. In truth, he dug out of the language all the pairings it contained.

On the one occasion when it failed him, he resorted to a device that no one can use after him. In the famous poem about Ruth and Boaz which is part of the quasi epic *La Légende des Siècles* (Saga of the Ages), the poet had a line that ended: . . . *et Ruth se demandait*, for which he

---

* *Réponse à un acte d'accusation* (1834) in *Les Contemplations*. The inevitable cultural lag can be measured by the fact that Laveaux's Dictionary of 1818, which indicates all words that are not "noble," was still being published in a revised edition in 1873.

needed a rime not only rich but appropriate to the setting. The riming line now reads:

Tout reposait dans Ur et dans Jérimadeth

That last place-name will not be found in any gazetteer; it is made up of the simple words *je rime à-dait*, the last syllable respelled to look like a Biblical name and the *je* endowed with an accent as it would be if such a foreign name had entered the language. It would also have lost in speech its final consonants, in accordance with the habits of the people, and thus it matches the verb ending that instigated the forgery.

In the textbooks that present Racine and Molière to French schoolchildren, a footnote recurs that says *"métaphore hardie"*—daring metaphor. By the time the course reaches the Romanticists the footnote has disappeared. It is steadily replaced by one that is needed to explain a succession of words as being not a misprint but a metaphor of a new type—obviously, since it needs a gloss. By this change one can measure the difference that the new century brought about in the character of literature and in the assumptions about the poet's duty to his art and his audience.

In the realm of images, this difference was largely the work of Hugo. Before him, even in Lamartine, the simile is the frequent form—"as when . . ." somebody or something acts in the manner to be described. In pure metaphor, which short-circuits resemblance by bringing together disparate words (the ship *ploughing* the sea), the Neo-classics had been restrained in part by the need for lucidity on the stage, in part by the niggling critics. Yet Racine and the others dotted their works with these *hardies* specimens later footnoted. By contrast, in Hugo's verse, imagery is virtually continuous, as in Shakespeare; it colors everything; nouns and adjectives are no longer literal; they connote: *les yeux sinistres de la lune; l'étoile n'est pas vraie;* verbs, too, succumb: *la nuit augmentait sur mon âme ravie; Il ressemblait au lys que sa blancheur défend;* it flourishes full strength in startling

---

All was peaceful in Ur and in Jerimadeth.

The *sinister* eyes of the moon / The star is not *true* / Night *increased upon* my delighted soul / He was like the lily whose whiteness *protects* [Mallarmé borrowed these last three words for his sonnet *Brise Marine.*] /

juxtapositions: *Secouant sur sa tête un haillon de lumière;* and in expanded form it fills two or more lines:

> Tous ces atomes las dont l'homme était le maître
> Sont joyeux d'être mis en liberté dans l'être,
> . . . .
> Le sang va retourner dans la veine infinie.

These three lines are part of a stream of images describing the dispersal of matter at death and its revivification in other material beings.

It is plain from everything Hugo wrote that he thought in images and that the often overwhelming, suffocating power of his poems is due to this gift of seeing: image succeeds image to re-present the initial experience or idea. Since these visions were original, hitherto unseen, they seemed to the poet equally entitled to a place in the total reality. It is therefore best to regard a long poem of his as a cluster of short ones on a given theme and to read no more than twenty, thirty lines at one sitting—or just ponder a couplet or quatrain; then return later for more. The result is refreshed wonder and pleasure, admiration and enthusiasm of the kind expressed by Flaubert, Gide, Pierre Louÿs, Valéry, Sartre, and others whose political views and artistic creed were the very opposite of Hugo's. Mallarmé himself would not allow his devotees to slight Hugo. °

The images I have quoted belong to the genre made commonplace by modern poets in all languages: they are not decoration, they stir more than one sense at a time, they flout reasonableness. In other words, they do not merely extend or magnify ordinary sight, as does the ship that ploughs the sea. Theoretically, any two perceptions can be linked through words when some underlying similarity (or contrast) occurs to the poet. Actually, every culture limits the choice, according to a principle that remains mysterious. Take the titles of books, many of which are half-grown metaphors; most of them are untranslatable: *A la recherche du temps perdu* or *Un homme se penche sur son passé*, if given correct dictionary equivalents, are disconcerting. In the

---

Shaking atop his head a *ragged sheaf of light*. (This head is that of the poet in general and Shakespeare's in particular.) All the weary atoms of which a man was the master / Are glad to be freed into being / . . . [His] blood will now return into the infinite vein.

former "lost time" is misleading; in the latter, a man's "leaning over his past" is absurd.

Here and in all images and epithets we see the wilfulness of language once more at work—and a further cause of untranslatability in poetry. English critics of French literature have often exclaimed at the silliness even of epithets in common locutions. One I happen to remember made merry over a novelist's *une après-midi adorable*—who can adore an afternoon? He might have been answered: "Tell us how the weather can be *glorious?*" which to a French ear verges on the idiotic.

The lesson to draw from this additional disparity between the two tongues is that learning to enjoy poetry in another language consists in becoming familiar, first, with the harmony and other resources of the meters, the rime schemes, the stanzas and kindred forms; and next, with the peculiar tendencies of its modifiers and images. These must be taken in direct, untranslated, like the titles of books. One more example to clinch the recommendation. Mallarmé's superb sonnet, *Brise Marine*, opens with the line:

La chair est triste, hélas! et j'ai lu tous les livres.

If mentally converted, the "sadness of the flesh" gets by, but "I have read all the books" totally lacks the evocative power of the original; as an image it is inert. An approximation would be: "and all knowledge is stale." The reason why the literal sense fails to convey this feeling lies in the aura of *livres;* the word is weightier, more charged with reverence than *books.* In "I've read all the books," one hears a schoolboy, not a philosopher.

In the reverse direction, a mind unused to English literature—not just to business speech—would balk at such images as "take arms against a sea of troubles" or "takes the winds of March with beauty." Utter nonsense, both of them, would be the verdict. And there is, beyond language, the individual sensibility, which will stretch only so far. Shakespeare could write: "the fringed curtains of thine eye advance," but most readers have thought it a poor figure to convey what is meant. ° For my part, I cannot read the much-admired song in *The Tempest,* "Full fathom five thy father lies," without revulsion. The vision of a corpse with coral growth in place of eyes and all the other "sea changes" affects me like bad surrealist horrors. Imagery, in

---

"Breeze from the Sea."

other words, is a perpetual risk, which is why the Neo-classics were timid about it—and also why at the hands of the Romanticists imagery extended the world of perception and reflection farther than had been done by any poets on record.

Reading Victor Hugo closely, but practicing temperance, is desirable for another reason. His range of subjects is very great. Despite Napoleon—or because of him—his themes are not purely national. They are drawn from the legends or history of every Western people and treated with equal sympathy. Hugo is a European poet, like Dante or Goethe. At the same time, in many of his poems he was obsessed by a small cluster of ideas: death, the deity, matter, and the immaterial or ideal world. The experience of love and the sight of nature made him joyful, exuberant, but there was death at the end of everything. Was there a God governing the magnificence of nature and seducing mankind with the enchantment of love? What kind of God, given the predominance of suffering, oppression, the prevailing lot of *les misérables?* And finally, since mind exists and implies a realm of immaterial being—spirit—what relation does it bear to the physical, the palpable reality that gives nature and love an irresistible grip on our lives?

Within this circle of unknowns, of contradictions, Hugo revolved endlessly. Wordsworth found an answer by attributing to Nature with a capital N the moral order and nurturing wisdom that he longed for. Hugo was less easily satisfied. He was torn between the revelations of the new sciences, which were preaching materialism, and the new (Hegelian) philosophy of Idealism, which made religion, art, and spirit a modern trinity at the expense of a personal, managerial God. Hugo at one moment thought that *La première faute / Fut le premier poids*—identifying error and sin with matter and gravitation. This equation suggests something like the formation of matter out of energy, if Blake is right and energy is the bodily, Satanic principle of life.

But at other times, Hugo thought that Nature—Pan—was the all-sufficing reality which should supersede in our minds the demand for a monarchical providence. In that tremendous cascade of images and actions *Le Satyre*, the bestial faun develops, attacks and, under the name of Pan, dethrones Jupiter. To the end of his life, Hugo wrestled with his own horrors and intuitions about the enigma, which endlessly brought into his verse the rimes *ombre* and *sombre*.

The first Sin / Was [at the same time] the first weight.

Once used to Hugo's ways with words, the reader will want to venture into other works than the contemplative. The plays should be read for the blend of the dramatic and the lyrical which was an innovation of the century—indeed, the hallmark of Romanticism—and which accounts for the failure of its best poets to write lasting plays. Shelley, Byron, Tennyson, Browning, Swinburne—and Hugo—all made the attempt and failed. In their lyrics the dramatic element is strong, recurrent, and must suffice.

Hugo also wrote contemporary satire. His caustic wit and virtuoso invective carry across the years, because he seized on the situation or the character trait that we recognize immediately without knowing the original circumstance. A whole collection of such poems directed against Napoleon III, *Les Châtiments*,* is made up of many different sorts of poems in different shapes and meters—sardonic ditties, some on old tunes; character sketches of politicians; brief dramatic scenes with or without dialogue; and longer descriptions, often aping the historical anecdote. A tremendous vision of the sort called "A Sewer in Rome" begins:

> Voici le trou, Voici l'échelle. Descendez.
> Tandis qu'au corps de garde en face on joue aux dés.
> En riant sous le nez des matrones bourrues,
>
> . . . .
>
> Vous voilà dans un lieu monstrueux, . . .
> Les durs barreaux de fer découpent le soleil, . . .

and after a catalogue of disgusting horrors, it concludes:

> Tout est fétide, informe, abject, terrible à voir.
>
> . . . .
>
> Sans pouvoir distinguer si ces mornes charognes

Here is the hole, here the ladder. Step down. / While in front of the barracks opposite the guards are rolling dice / And laugh under the nose of the huffy matrons. . . . / You find yourself in a monstrous place . . . / The stark iron bars cut the sun into pieces. . . . / Everything is fetid, misshapen, abject, dreadful to see . . . / And nobody can tell if these dejected carcases /

*The literal term is "Chastisements"; better would be: "Whips and Scorpions."

Ont une forme encor visible en leurs débris
Et sont des chiens crevés ou des césars pourris.

These "castigations" of the dictatorship are one of the reasons for Hugo's periodic acclaim by democratic France: he stands as the voice of the first *Résistance* and re-appears, to those who have denigrated him since his death, as not so passé after all. But in other periods, this concern with popular feelings and causes lead his detractors to call Hugo stupid. It makes one more bond with Wordsworth, whose poetry, said one critic, is at times sublime, and at other times "the voice of a half-witted sheep."°

Because the general tenor of the anti-Hugo charges is familiar enough abroad to have virtually excluded him from the ranks of the great poets, notice of it must be taken before we move on to his fellow Romanticists. The put-down is expressed in capsule form in André Gide's supposed reply to someone who inquired who was the greatest French poet: "Victor Hugo, alas!" It is a clever repartee, except that it never happened and that its point is missed. Had it been said, it would assert, with no matter what cause of regret, that Hugo *is* the greatest French poet. Actually, the words were never spoken. When young and a fervent Symbolist, Gide filled out a questionnaire in a literary review that asked: "Who is your poet?" (meaning favorite). Gide wrote *"Hugo, hélas,"* enjoying no doubt the brevity and the alliteration.°

Throughout the half-century following that answer, Gide continued to read, recite, and comment on Hugo with perceptive enthusiasm. He knew much of his work by heart. The *Journals* tell us what he admired and why—that is, why Hugo *was* the greatest French poet—and also why the *hélas*. The praise persists after a succession of other great poets—Baudelaire, Rimbaud, Verlaine, Heredia, Valéry—had earned fame and were vividly present to Gide's mind. To the end, Hugo remained for Gide *le père de la poésie moderne.* ° Having reread *Les Orientales*, an early collection, Gide writes: "Everything is there—strength, grace, a smile, and the most moving sobs. What resourcefulness! What a poetic earthquake! What a play of technique in his versification! Such mastery and ease is achieved only by yielding

---

Still keep some form among the parts / And are the bodies of dead dogs or of rotting Caesars. ("L'Egoût de Rome," *Les Châtiments*, VII, 4)

completely to the suggestiveness of words and their sounds. This subordinates the idea to the word and to the image, and explains why Hugo, by no means stupid as he is often called, preferred a commonplace emotion or idea, that he might devote himself entirely to the physical pleasure of expressing it, of letting it develop and spread forth."°

That physical pleasure came from the poet's ear attuned to the subtleties of verbal sound. We know from his own words how Hugo regarded his vocabulary: "Each word is in itself a small orchestra in which the vowel is the voice and the consonant the instrument, the accompaniment—*sonat cum* (it sounds with)."°

That with this means his larger "orchestration" was unrivalled, nobody who knows the language has ever denied. But that qualifier— knowing the language—is essential, as the Irish poet and novelist George Moore pointed out to his English confrères. Moore had been living in Paris for some years and was about to introduce to England the new, brash Impressionist painters, when he wrote his *Confessions of a Young Man*. In it he challenges the "negative dogma" I detailed in the first pages of this essay. "I feel," says Moore, "that it is almost impossible for the same ear to seize music so widely differing as Milton's blank verse and Hugo's alexandrines, and it seems to me especially strange that critics varying in degree from Matthew Arnold to the obscure paragraphist never seem even remotely to suspect, when they passionately declare that English blank verse is a more perfect and complete poetic instrument than French alexandrines, that the imperfections which they aver are inherent in the latter exist only in their British ears, impervious to a thousand subtleties. Mr. Matthew Arnold does not hesitate to say that the regular rhyming of lines is monotonous. To my ear every line is different; there is as much variation in Charles V's soliloquy as in Hamlet's."°

With his extraordinary mimetic ear, Swinburne composed a pastiche that confirms this view. He wrote French prose with occasional lapses from idiom, but his imitation of Victor Hugo in the poem "Charenton en 1810" is so perfect in diction, tone, and imagery that it could pass for a piece from *La Légende des Siècles*. Its one hundred sixteen lines, also a soliloquy, portray the Marquis de Sade; it has all Hugo's love of realistic detail, seemingly irrelevant but suggestive of life bustling around the main figure, and all the variety of line that Moore responded to: it was there to be imitated.

Il marchait l'oeil voilé, fauve; et toute Sodome
Vivait, rêvait, brûlait, hurlait dans ce grand homme.

Swinburne knew French poetry from the time of Villon to his
own, and his indignation, similar to Moore's, also prompted an angry
essay against "the cherished dogma of English faith that French verse
is wanting in the supreme musical and delightful qualities of metre:
that the most lyrical of languages (for the English and the Italian are
both in comparison over facile and slippery, while in French there is
no safe walking for any but a strong and faultless master of sound and
form—here a man may do decently and passably; there he must do
absolutely well or ill), that this noble and subtle lyric instrument is
unfit for lyric use."° And again catching up Arnold, who missed in
French verse the pleasure of simple, lilting song, Swinburne quotes a
stanza from Musset and then one from Gautier:

> Menez-moi, dit la belle
> A la rive fidèle
>   Où l'on aime toujours.
> Cette rive, ma chère,
> On ne la connaît guère
>   Au pays des amours.

The judgments on record in these delicate matters must be
weighed, not counted; and these last two that I have chosen must be
remembered as going beyond Hugo to the "cherished dogma" of
English critics about French poetry. Hugo was a good argument to
use. Looking back in 1870 on forty-five years of Hugo's work in verse
before writing his theory of French poetic technique, Théodore de
Banville had no doubt that here was the consummate artist who not
only restored the language to its pristine scope and vigor, but who

---

He stalked with eyes veiled, feral; and the soul of Sodom/Lived,
dreamed, burned, howled in this great man. (Lines 51–52.) As reprinted, a
circumflex appears on *Sodome* that has no business there. If in the original, it
is Swinburne's only mistake.

Take me, said the charmer/To the faithful clime/Where love is for-
ever./Ah, That clime, my dear/Has never been found/In the land of love.
("Barcarolle," last stanza. Berlioz chose the poem as one of six Gautier songs
to form the lyric suite *Nuits d'Eté.*)

also exemplified the whole art of French versification. "It is all contained in one volume," says Banville, *"La Légende des Siècles*. It should be the Bible of every French poet. . . . To read Hugo competently is to learn all there is to know about verse."°

Hugo mastered every form, from the Malayan *pantoum* (which he introduced) to the ode and the epical narrative—except the sonnet— and he developed several, notably playing variations on the stanza made up of one, two, three, four, or five alexandrines with a half-line close:

> J'aime les soirs sereins et beaux, j'aime les soirs,
> Soit qu'ils dorent le front des antiques manoirs
>> Ensevelis dans les feuillages;
> Soit que la brume au loin s'allonge en bancs de feu,
> Soit que mille rayons brisent dans un ciel bleu
>> A des archipels de nuages.

The half line in these various combinations both keeps the alexandrines from becoming solemn and permits the conclusion of the meaning to be strong or gentle, a comment or an image, or even not a conclusion at all, but a pivot on which the theme can take a new direction in the succeeding lines.

As for meters, the old catholicity of French verse, by which lines of every length from two to twelve syllables were deemed appropriate to one or another use, was rehabilitated in this same period, by all the Romanticists together. In so doing, they looked even farther back than the sixteenth century, whose Pléïade they invoked as models and precedents for their *hardiesses*.° Hugo, with characteristic daring and a sure hand, used nine of these twelve meters in one poem, omitting the alexandrine. *Les Djinns* warrants this tour de force by its subject matter, and since it displays the range, tone, and rhythmical features of these principal meters, I have reproduced it at the end of this essay, with an "approximation" of my own in rimed English.

Much later, in his sixties, Hugo brought out a collection of lyrics in which there is not a single alexandrine: *Chansons des rues et des bois.*

I love those evenings serene and fair, evenings / Such as gild the face of ancient manor houses / Buried in foliage / Or when the far-off haze stretches in banks of fire / Or when a thousand rays in a blue sky break against / Archipelagos of clouds. ("Soleils couchants," *Les Feuilles d'automne*, XXXV)

Most of the quatrains are in eight syllables, the others in four, five, six, and ten, with one piece in lines that alternate seven and three syllables. And the mood throughout is hedonistic, full of sensual gaiety. Writing *Les Misérables* just previously had doubtless brought on a reaction toward love of nature and joie de vivre.

The sonnet, I said above, was the one form Hugo did not make his own. It was obviously too narrow a frame for the visionary to look through and find the material for song or myth. It was left to Musset to use it in original fashion—short lines, light subjects tinged with pathos or irony, *plus* the qualities of the form in its primary intention: a message to the beloved. In his own sphere, Musset is as masterly a poet as Hugo. Poetry poured out of him too: songs, satirical tales, meditations, invective, playlets, elegies, and epistles. He was accused of carelessness in rime, and even in the count of syllables, but these *négligences*—conscious for the most part—do not mar his music or his fluid solidity and accurate imagery. Like his fellow Romanticists, he did not tolerate filler—*la cheville;* he voiced their credo in the strongest terms:

> Le dernier des humains est celui qui cheville

A *cheville* is a wedge, pin, dowel, plug, shim, or other piece of wood cut to fill a hole or gap. In the technique of verse it means a word or phrase thought up to complete a line when the idea has been adequately expressed without taking up all the room between rimes. The poet plugs the gap with an adjective or clause that adds nothing to the meaning, and probably nothing to the harmony either, since the choice of words is constrained by the space and the grammar of the line. A *vers chevillé* discloses its cobbled character at sight:

> Mais dès qu'on veut tenter cette vaste carrière,
> Pégase s'effarouche et recule en arrière

Since *recule* means "goes backward" and *en arrière* means "backwards" one or the other is padding. The rime was perhaps too good to let go, but the price of keeping it was rather high.

He who pads his verses is the lowest of creatures. (*Après une lecture*, XVI)

Boileau, *"Au roi"*: As soon as one seeks to make this great attempt/ Pegasus takes umbrage and goes backward backwards.

In English, "does" (or "doth") often serves as *cheville* to assist the meter: "Every wise man's son doth know" (*Twelfth Night*). In French, owing to the lack of fixed accents, it is particularly important to make *vers pleins* ("full"—of meaning) as Musset insisted, because padding, by its deficiency or redundancy of sense, causes the rhythm to flag: there is no proper indication of where to lay the slight stress that sustains the voice—not to mention the opportunity missed through failing to use the vacant syllables to enrich significance or add to the imagery. This is where Musset by natural gift and Hugo by settled habit excel. Both use the line to give, without let-up, what Banville called *le plein de l'idée*, the fullness of the thought.

It might be objected, of course, that fullness can be excessive. When given too much to absorb in every line of a long poem, the reader's eye, ear, and imagination succumb and enjoyment declines. This view is part of the charge against Hugo, as well as the reason for my recommendation to read him in small portions. For with him, even expressions that would not be condemned as *chevilles* are replaced by still more pregnant terms, visual or intellectual. For example:

> Les mélèzes
> Font au loin un bruit vague au penchant des falaises.

Here not only have the trees their proper name, but the verse indicates distance, sound, and place, specifying in addition the *slope* of the cliffs. Had he written "*bruit vague* ET QUI VIENT *des falaises*" or some such wording, nobody would have thought the line *chevillée*. In this *au penchant* is the clue to Romanticist poetics, born of the passion for experience. It is not surprising to learn that Valéry remarked on this fact; to the very last, he said, Hugo's lines had been as full as lines can be made.* Valéry's own method is akin to Hugo's in its concentration, image crowding upon image in each line. Both poets compel the reader to unwind the numerous strands that the poet has made not so much into a line as into a rope. This unwinding is fa-

---

The larches / Make a vague noise far off on the slope of the cliffs. ("L'aigle du casque" from *La Légende des Siècles*)

* Valéry's actual words show that he was thinking of specific features: "What prodigious lines, lines to which no others can be compared for scope, for internal organization, for resonance, for fullness did he not write in the last period of his life!" (*Variété II*, Paris, 1930, 153)

miliar work to the reader of modern poetry. The only reason he neglects to do the same for Hugo is that in the precursor of the technique there is still discursive tissue that makes one believe a whole page can be read running-fashion, like prose. A slower pace and some reflection would change the reader's sense of excess into admiration and pleasure.

With Musset, no such effort seems necessary. His forte, on the contrary, is (as I said) fluidity, which offers the option of reading at a run. But that ease and elegance may be deceptive; it conceals the art, to begin with, and it also conceals the seriousness of the thought. *Namouna*, for instance, is a conversational tale in the manner of Byron's *Don Juan*, and at first it promises chiefly social satire. But it modulates, often and rapidly, and one collides (as it were) with such things as:

> Et la preuve, lecteur, la preuve irrécusable
> Que ce monde est mauvais, c'est que, pour y rester,
> Il a fallu s'en faire un autre, et l'inventer.
> Un autre!—monde étrange, absurde, inhabitable,
> Et qui, pour valoir mieux que le seul véritable,
> N'a pas même un instant eu besoin d'exister.

In this rapid narrative, some fifty pages long, one finds nearly all the themes Musset treated in various forms during his relatively brief career: love betrayed by the perverse will on either side; the haunting thought of death; the obsessive question of the existence of God, the answer to it being now yes, now no; and the supreme delight and infinite worth of poetry:

> Elle a cela pour elle
> Que les sots d'aucun temps n'en ont pu faire cas,
> Qu'elle nous vient de Dieu—qu'elle est limpide et belle,
> Que le monde l'entend, et ne la parle pas.

And the proof, reader, the irrefutable proof, / That this world is bad, is that to endure it / Another has had to be made—sheer invention / Another world! Strange, absurd, and unlivable / But which to be better than the only real one / Did not even for one moment have to exist. (*Namouna*, I, 50)

One of her merits is / That fools in any age have had no use for her, / That she is from God—and as beautiful as she is pure / That the world understands her speech—and does not speak it. / (Ibid., II, 2)

It is in fact Musset's characteristic to turn his inspiration from whatever source to the uses, in succession, of humor, grief, eroticism, and religious uncertainty. In his youthful "Ballad to the Moon," which begins

> C'était dans la nuit brune
> Sur le clocher jauni,
>   La lune
> Comme un point sur un i.

the vision changes from charm to derision of the moon's face; it becomes ugly and eaten away with the march of time; it turns next into a signal of damnation, and again into a face looking like a cynical witness of love troubles. Musset's prevailing mood is despair, no matter what may come before it or after:

> Partout où j'ai voulu dormir,
> Partout où j'ai voulu mourir,
> Partout où j'ai touché la terre,
> Sur ma route est venu s'asseoir
> Un malheureux vêtu de noir
> Qui me ressemblait comme un frère.

Anyone reading Musset at some length needs no footnotes to point out the constant presence of the natural fused with the unexpected and held within a tight-knit, harmonious unity. If Hugo's verse feels as if wrought on the forge, Musset's is liquid metal cast in a mold. His art belongs to the tradition that goes back to Marot and includes Molière and La Fontaine. Nor is this permanent readiness in Musset limited to poems in a low key: he commands the grand style too, as one may see in the elegy on the death of the singer Maria-Felicia García. To tear out a piece of it for quotation would be a sacrilege. It has all the calm indignation, all the resonant finality of *Lycidas* or *Adonais*.

The same gift of unforced solemnity was bestowed on Musset's

It was in the dun night / On the yellowed spire / The moon / Like the dot on an i. (*Ballade à la lune*)

Wherever I have wished to sleep, / Wherever I have wished to die, / Wherever I have set foot on earth, / On my way there came and sat with me / A hapless wretch all dressed in black / Who was as like myself as a brother. (*Nuit de Décembre*)

older contemporary, Alfred de Vigny, but not the same power of versification. His very character of stoical self-control probably inhibited articulateness; few of his poems, at any rate, are without weak or confused lines—and not for want of care: Vigny published nothing between 1835 and his death twenty-eight years later, and only then did some of his finest poems first appear.

Their subjects, historical, religious, or contemporary, afforded him occasions for asserting or implying that in a world governed by chance and predominantly evil, the sole duty of man is silent resignation. To bear the burdens of life and die without complaint is the theme of the magnificent *Mort du Loup*. To regard poetry and science as mankind's sole redeeming activities is the lesson in the moving parable, *La Bouteille à la mer*. The former would be perfect except for one *cheville: Sa retraite est coupée et tous ses chemins pris;* the rest is concentrated drama, tense emotion, inspired imagery.

Every thought arises naturally from the story of a wolf hunt. The darkness, the tracks of the animals in the sand, the anxious hunters with drawn knives pushing aside the underbrush and stepping cautiously, create a magical scene. Suddenly:

> J'aperçois tout à coup deux yeux qui flamboyaient,
> Et je vois au delà quatre formes légères
> Qui dansaient sous la lune au milieu des bruyères.

The male wolf shields his mate and offspring and is mortally wounded,

> Et sans daigner savoir comment il a péri,
> Refermant ses grands yeux, meurt sans jeter un cri.

The other poem is dramatic in another way—indeed, nearly all Vigny's descriptive poems are condensed dramas, the characteristic form of the age. The flask is thrown into the sea by the captain of a

---

"The Death of the Wolf." / "The flask thrown into the sea."

His retreat is cut off and all roads are blocked.

All at once I catch sight of a pair of glowing eyes / And beyond, I see four light-footed forms / That were dancing in the moonlight amid the heather.

And not concerned to know how he has come to die / But closing his great eyes, gives up the ghost without a cry.

ship that has struck an uncharted reef and is sinking: he puts what he has learned and the position of the reef into the bottle, which he hopes will be cast ashore and bring his knowledge to other men. The poem looks back to the lives and hopes of the gallant explorers and then turns to the journey of the floating bottle, a series of vivid imaginings, including a brush with pirates, whose presence scares away the ship about to rescue the flask. It floats on,

> Seule dans l'Océan, seule toujours!—Perdue
> Comme un point invisible en un mouvant désert, . . .

Safe at the end, its odyssey prompts the lesson

> Le vrai Dieu, le Dieu fort est le Dieu des idées.

To Vigny, ideas were indeed paramount and, though he was a linguist, the art of versifying did not tempt him to invent new forms or play variations on the old. The alexandrine suited most of his meditations, words did not sing wild tunes in his heart. More than Musset or Hugo, he had been adversely affected in childhood by revolution and war. In adult life he was beset by sorrows and unremitting duties toward his ailing mother and wife. Family tradition made of him a professional soldier for a time, but the realities of peacetime service gave no scope to his desire for glory, only for his sense of responsibility. So after success in prose fiction and plays, he retired to his modest estate, where he could enjoy nature:

> Silence des rochers, des vieux bois et des plaines,
> Calme majestueux des murs noirs et des tours,
> Vaste immobilité des ormes et des chênes,
> Lente uniformité de la nuit et des jours,
> Solennelle épaisseur des horizons sauvages,
> Roulis aérien des nuages de mer. . . .

Alone in the ocean, alone forever.—Lost / Like an invisible spot in a shifting desert, . . .

The true God, the strong God, is the God of Thought.

Silence of rocks and ancient woods and plains, / Majestic calm of blackened walls and towers, / Grand immobility of elms and oaks, / Slow uniformity of nights and days, / Solemn thickness of wild horizons, / Rolling waves of airborne clouds above the sea . . . (Posthumous fragment)

The last two of the Romanticist Pléïade (if one takes Chénier as the first of the seven) give the impression of being less innovators than links between these and those about to come ushering in a change of tone. Yet this pair, Gautier and Nerval, cannot be called poets of a younger generation. Closest of friends, they were born within the same dozen years as the others, and they defended Romanticism, shared its perceptions and beliefs, and practiced its techniques, though they did not help create it.

Their forward-looking contributions were a product of temperament. Gautier, besides being a poet, novelist, and critic, was for a time a painter. He was always aware—in his own words—of "being a man for whom the visible world exists." He had a keen sense of color and plasticity and in a collection of poems, *Emaux et Camées*, published at the mid-century and setting forth his *art poétique*, he proclaimed the need for verse once more to adopt the principle of "difficulty overcome." From it would arise a severe, sculptured beauty whose products would outlast the civilization itself:

> Oui, l'oeuvre sort plus belle
> D'une forme au travail
> Rebelle,
> Vers, marbre, onyx, émail.
> . . . .
> Tout passe—L'art robuste
> Seul a l'éternité,
> Le buste
> Survit à la cité.

In his prose criticism, Gautier never repudiated Romanticism or its masters, who were also his friends; but the truly next generation of poets chose to separate him, praising his example of spare versification. Baudelaire dedicated *Les Fleurs du Mal* to Gautier with the words "impeccable poet, perfect magician, master and friend." Leconte de Lisle and the so-called Parnassians adopted—as they believed from Gautier—the creed of objective creation, of detachment from the introspective self, even at the cost of a certain coldness. It was a turning away from the dazzling ease and force of Hugo and the personal confidences of Musset, from abundance and individuality.

Yes: the work comes forth fairer / From a form that against the hand / Resists / Be it verse, marble, gem, ceramic. . . . / All things perish—Sturdy art / Alone has eternity / A bust / Survives a city. (*L'Art*)

The Romanticists, morever, had engendered many imitators—*tout le monde faisait du Hugo*. As Banville pointed out, their new poetics had been turned into a set of recipes and formulas. The reaction was primarily against these, and the only form it could take was austerity, a sort of classicism, in the conventional sense of calm, "rigor," and impersonality; of conscious withdrawal from the battle of ideas to cultivate art in the pure state. "Pure poetry," or "Art for art's sake," is a recurrent ideal after periods of *engagement* (commitment) to social and other worldly causes. It was the new slogan to which Gautier gave currency without intending to start a new school of poetry.

By contrast, Nerval's originality lay in giving intimations of a secret self moving in a mysterious ideal world. His temperament was compounded of commonplace jocularity—he was fond of hoaxing—and dark anxiety leading to periodic depressions, during the last of which he committed suicide. He was a traveller, learned German and read mystical works in that language, collected the folk songs of his native province, and wrote prose fiction about vaporous creatures and their experience of the indefinite. His small body of poetry is renowned for the few poems in which the later Symbolists said they found the pattern of their thought and verbal methods. The most famous of these poems is the sonnet *El Desdichado*. Its first line sets the mood, or better, the moodiness

Je suis le ténébreux,—le veuf,—l'inconsolé

and the remaining thirteen form a riddle as to what exactly the poet means: the speaker is a prince deprived of "his tower" and also of "his star"—his love; he addresses her consoling shade (she is in the grave) to restore to him a variety of joys. Then, at the turn from the octet, he questions his own identity and the last six lines contain apparently discontinuous ideas. The reader makes up his own interpretation of each and of all together.

Not the Symbolists alone, but critics of our century, in their loathing of the Romanticists, have asserted that this sonnet and another called *Daphné*, equally suggestive and imprecise, are the only two poems worth attention in the entire half-century after the death of Chénier. One French anthologist gives more space to Nerval than to Hugo; a more recent English one, who devoutly embraces seven

---

I am the dark-minded one, the bereft, the unconsoled. (*El Desdichado* means "The Unfortunate.")

centuries of French poetry, again gives four pages to Nerval and two to Hugo, three pages to Musset and six lines to Lamartine. Believers in "pure poetry" naturally prefer Nerval even to Gautier, because in Gautier the references to the outer world that he cherished are at all times perfectly clear.

But there are dissenters from this extreme. Gide in *his* anthology grudgingly gives Nerval's two sonnets and says: "I have made repeated efforts—vain efforts—to develop a warm feeling for Gérard de Nerval. I should like to be able to admire the writings of this charming and delicate mind. . . . Unfortunately, the most prosaic sort of reasoning invariably turns up in his work to buttress his wandering reason. Everything in these much touted sonnets is contrived, rationally worked out, done on purpose. [Others], over generously, find in them all that Nerval tried to put in and that to my regret I cannot *feel* there."°

Nerval himself laid no claim to having innovated. In the dedication of the volume containing "El Desdichado," he speaks of it as "one of the sonnets composed in the dream-state the Germans call Super-naturalist. . . . [These pieces] are hardly more obscure than the metaphysics of Hegel or the writings of Swedenborg, and they would lose all their charm if they were explained—assuming such a thing to be possible. Give me credit, at least, for the mode of expression."°

Neither Nerval nor Gautier, rear-guard representatives of Roman-ticism, would have claimed for a moment a place among creators such as later-comers have assigned them. Gautier always regarded Hugo as The Master, and Nerval versified his own poetic debt to him in a dozen lines ending:

Et que mon peu de feu s'allume à vos autels

———————

And [I know] that my modest fire is kept alight at your altar. ("A Victor Hugo," *Poésies diverses*)

~§ VIII §~

Take eloquence and wring its neck.
—Verlaine, *Art Poétique* (1873)

Two things besides fatigue account for the radical shift in outlook away from Romanticism and for the extraordinary animus, the angry revulsion, the indignant scorn with which the next generations treated the movement. One is the revolutions of 1848; the other is the collapse of philosophy from an inadequate idealism into a crude materialism. Poets have no obligation to be philosophers and few of them read philosophy, but most if not all absorb the new doctrines in the air of their time and these affect their work, both the contents and the form, as we shall abundantly see.

1848 in France and its four-year sequel of uprisings all over Europe toppled thrones, caused repression, civil wars, executions, and ex-iles, and finally brought on an eighteen-year dictatorship under a nephew of Napoleon in the country where Liberal democracy had first sought to establish itself. Those events broke the back of the century culturally and emotionally. Many artists died or fled from their homelands, promising careers were ruined, and perhaps worst of all, intellectuals were discredited on the one hand and disillusioned on the other.

Every generous idea previously accepted was now despised, and in fact blamed for failure to bring about the better world. Love, liberty, progress, the sovereign people, the brotherhood of man, and the oneness of spirit under a mysterious but manifest providence—these were now regarded as the vaporings of feeble minds or glib rhetori-cians. What was true was hard matter and evil man, nothing else. Science confirmed the first of these only realities, politics the other. Hence Realism and Materialism: "Things are in the saddle And ride mankind."°

Realism, moreover, was defined as the commonplace, the dull, dreary, sordid, repetitious occurrences of daily life. They made anything other than soberness of word and feeling ridiculous. To be sure, the Romanticists had often felt despair; they were not fools—or blind. But their love of life was strong, and they were also gifted with the love of love; those among them who survived the debacle of '48 kept their faith in humankind and felt it a duty to continue the fight for political freedom and social equality. Hugo, exiled on his

Channel Island for eighteen years, was the chief spokesman for this "Nevertheless" attitude and thereby earned the contempt of the younger men who *knew* that ideas were "mere" ideas and worthless. He continued to love and worship nature; they, on the contrary, were possessed by the emotion that Roger Williams has described and analyzed in his book *The Horror of Life* and has shown by psychological and medical evidence to have been no affectation but fact. °

The future is always the work of the young among survivors; the horror of life was bound to prevail over hope and the vision of a new Jerusalem. I am speaking here of culture—mood, tone, and forms of expression; the political battle, under and above ground, is another story. I mentioned earlier the name Parnassians. It comes from a periodical, *Le Parnasse Contemporain*, which from 1866 on published the poets that set the new standards. Their leader was Leconte de Lisle and their creed was "objectivity." The poet was to see and describe—a kind of scientist—keeping his feelings and notions to himself. As Leconte put it in a sonnet called *Les Montreurs* (The Exhibitionists), writers who give away their emotions and opinions are to be classed with mountebanks and prostitutes (*les histrions et les prostituées*). Hugo, Musset, Lamartine, please take note.

But what was the true kind of poem to contain? Leconte gave the answer in his *Poèmes antiques*, *Poèmes barbares*, and *Poèmes tragiques*. I quoted above a few lines from him in discussing harmony in verse: the subjects are chiefly scenes from history, distant in time or remote in space. Insight into the mind is not excluded, but the mind is that of somebody other than the poet. As if to make his point even plainer, Leconte took up the learned fad of spelling Greek and other foreign terms "correctly." *Clytemnestre* written *Klytaemnestra* and words such as *houri* and *houkah* transmogrified into *hûri* and *hûka* supposedly established distance and scientific scholarship.

In form, the changes from Hugo-esque technique are matters of degree: rimes are sometimes less rich, to be less conspicuous, the rhythm more sedate, and the images make a shorter leap from reality. Leconte's versification may be called a return to Chénier by way of Vigny. The detachment is more in the manner than the substance:

> Homme, si, le coeur plein de joie ou d'amertume,
> Tu passais vers midi dans les champs radieux,

O man! if with a heart full of joy or bitterness / You should at noontime cross the radiant fields, /

> Fuis! La nature est vide et le soleil consume:
> Rien n'est vivant ici, rien n'est triste ou joyeux.

That here was no counter-revolution in artistry is evident from the interesting fact that Banville, whom we have heard worshipping Hugo, was one of the older Parnassians. And his light ironic verse, brilliant in technique, exquisite in detail, and subdued in lyric impulse, plainly shows that the fervor of an earlier day had vanished.

But human passion—especially in poets—is not to be turned on and off like a tap. In this grim period of the mid-nineteenth century, it burst out in *Les Fleurs du Mal*, the perfect expression of "the horror of life." The poet himself, in his dedication, calls his poems *"ces fleurs maladives,"* which means not so much sickly flowers as "flowers of sickness." Baudelaire's technique remains that of the Romanticists; it is in his appearance of "objectivity" that he is connected with the Parnassians.

The novelty of his book resides in a triple contrast: the express desire for *ordre et beauté, Luxe, calme et volupté;* descriptions of sordidness or vice linked with love or ideal yearnings; and, in manner, a deliberate deadness in the utterance, a drugged quality in the rhythm, matched in the riming by attempts at richness that often fail. Indeed, flaccid or banal polysyllables at the end of the second line of a couplet suggest the need to avoid eloquence. The truth is, Baudelaire found riming difficult; he pairs the same type or form of words or is often content with what is hardly more than assonance. He uses inversion to avoid rhythmic difficulties at the cesura, and his vocabulary is scanty. Where he innovates is in making these limitations, purposeful or not, serve the intent to make memorable poetry by reproducing the ghastly reality, the ubiquitous prose. What Hugo and Musset used for special effects turns into a style. Faults and merits in Baudelaire beautifully come together to communicate that unmistakable atmosphere of the new realism, of experience narrowed by unhappiness, which the age took on as its character.

The alexandrine is Baudelaire's prevailing line (in one hundred

---

Flee! Nature is a void and the sun burns away: / Nothing here is alive, nothing sad or joyful. ("Midi,"*Poèmes antiques*)

Order and Beauty, / The sumptuous, repose, and the voluptuous. ("L'Invitation au voyage")

thirty-one out of one hundred sixty-seven pieces) and he freely mixes the binary and ternary meters in the same verse:

Pourtant, qui n'a serré dans ses bras un squelette. . . .

The first accent comes at the comma and the next at the ninth and twelfth syllables, but the regular cesura at the sixth is still perceptible; the line just "hesitates" in the middle.

Among forms, Baudelaire exploits the sonnet, also in alexandrines, where his design of juxtaposing fair and foul stands out with violent effect. His whole output is violent, like his nature. He fired one shot at random in the revolution of 1848 and tried in vain to gather a squad who would join him in killing the stepfather he hated. That was all the fury he expressed physically. But in his verse, the very succession of titles in his book shows his repressed rage: Hymn to Beauty; A Rotting Carcass; Love and the Skull; Elevation; The Sick Muse; Journey to Cythera; The Barrel of Hatred. I cite at random, but the hate turned inward is evident; it appears again in the suicidal moments of his life early and late.

In the poetry it produced those sudden turns for which he is famous: a ten-line address to his mistress begins by calling her "a vessel of sadness" and ends by comparing his erotic exertions upon her to the onslaught of "a chorus of worms upon a cadaver." In turn, this comparison bespeaks "her coldness, which to him makes her the more beautiful."° Like all the post-Romantics, Baudelaire is a specialist. He works with but a few images and exploits three or four recurring themes.

In reading Baudelaire, one soon discovers another trait that marks the break with the past: his world is urban. He takes pains to point out that the great forests frighten him; he hates the ocean, because it reminds him of his own inner tumult and shows

. . . l'homme vaincu, plein de sanglots et d'insultes

The city it is that gives rise to the comprehensive word for the unrelieved Baudelairian experience: "Spleen." Its connotation in

---

Yet whoever has not clasped in his arms a skeleton. . . .

. . . Man defeated, full of tears and loaded with insults.

French is depression; it is not tender like melancholy, nor does it carry the idea of resentment as does English "spleen." The soul is weary; every small accident underscores the hopeless, meaningless, and unchangeable character of human life; whence the horror of it. Here is the opening of the first of the three famous "Spleen" poems:

> J'ai plus de souvenirs que si j'avais mille ans.
> Un gros meuble à tiroirs encombré de bilans,
> De vers, de billets doux, de procès, de romances,
> Avec de lourds cheveux roulés dans des quittances,
> Cache moins de secrets que mon triste cerveau.

The other two begin, respectively, with: "I am like the king of a rainy country;" and "When the sky is low and heavy like a lid."

No doubt is left about the moral climate in which everything in Baudelaire's world takes place. The clearings in this dark weather come in the form of *imagined* relief, longed for, and not for a moment to be thought real. "L'Invitation au voyage" is but a dream; "Beauty" exists only in the minds of poets; and the "ideal being" for *this* poet is explicitly a fierce "red ideal," none other than Lady Macbeth, because she is capable of crime; or else Michelangelo's figure, "Night of the Tomb" in Florence, who "sleeps in a strange posture," her physical attractions "fashioned by the mouths of Titans."

All these images, these mixed desires, coupled with erotic experiences both voluptuous and sordid, explain why Baudelaire has become for many English readers the first French poet they admire after Villon. Baudelaire satisfies the hatred of modern society felt by sensitive natures, and he records the fruitless yearnings that seem to be best expressed in poetry by more or less explicit reference to sexuality and its perversions.

This aspect of *Les Fleurs du Mal* is discreet enough by twentieth-century standards; it was outrageous by nineteenth, and it qualified the book for prosecution in the courts. What aggravated the offense was the rather complacent expression of remorse sheltering under the religious doctrine of fallen man. This combination too, of enormities described with a varnish of religiosity added, became a leading motif of subsequent literature down to the present.

I remember more things than if I were a thousand years old. / A large bureau with many drawers full of balance sheets, / Verses, love letters, lawsuits, and parlor songs / With heavy tresses rolled up in receipted bills / Contains fewer secrets than my sorry brain. (*Fleurs du Mal*, LXXVI, LXXVII and LXVIII)

In retrospect, the work of the Parnassians, crowned by Baudelaire's achievement, appears as what I have called specialization. The new school took from the Romanticists not only verse technique, but also whatever else in their work it found congenial, adaptable to their spiritually crushed condition—despair, stoicism, love cynically flouted, images of violence and sordidness, compassion for the downtrodden. By concentrating the dose, the effect was made overwhelming and seemed a new departure. Hugo was the first to acknowledge it when he said of Baudelaire that he had created *le frisson nouveau*—the new thrill—this in no disparaging sense. By affirming an antisocial attitude, it was indeed new—it was alienation declared by the poet for the benefit of all who have the wit to feel the horror of life and to see through the fallacy of progress.

For yet another cause of unhappiness was the encroachment of machine industry and its attendant uglification of town and country. The Romanticists had sung in an agrarian civilization; *towns* were for handiwork and commerce. Industry made the *city*, bringing in not factories only, and railroads, but also slums, crowds, a new type of filth, and shoddy goods, commonly known as "cheap and nasty." And when free public schools were forced on the nation by the needs of industry, a further curse was added: the daily paper, also cheap.

This last item sounds like a tired joke, but one must read Baudelaire to see how seriously it is to be taken. The newspaper was his bête noire; he railed at it, called it Satanic. He loathed it not as a symbol but as a fact and a force. The reason for this animus was that the penny paper created what has since been called the mass mind. The schools, by teaching reading and writing, produced the halfeducated; and *their* newspaper—its language, clichés, "sensations," and illustrations—kept the populace in the state of vulgarity and opinionativeness that forever prevented their becoming civilized.

The poet, the artist, was thereby displaced, even in his own eyes. He was no longer the hero, the seer and prophet who leads a grateful people to a higher spiritual life. He was now an outcast—*maudit* (accursed), doomed to misery, poverty, disease, and death. Baudelaire celebrates wine and opium and women as providers of *paradis artificiels*. From his day onward it has been the expected thing that artists should end not triumphant in palaces but outcast in the charity hospital and the pauper's grave.

The contradiction of the superior man in the inferior place heightens the disgust with self, while at the same time it reveals as part of the artist's resentment the ambition for high status and power. The upshot in poetry is the paradox of compassion expressed for "the people" and hostility to democracy and its material betterment. Thus, in one of his *Little Poems in Prose* Baudelaire speaks of the pleasures of "taking a bath in the populace. To enjoy the crowd is an art." His urban intelligence perceives that "multitude and solitude— it is all one."° But in another such prose poem entitled "Let us beat up the poor," Baudelaire tells a parable about economic and social equality: no one is entitled to it; it belongs to those who can win it and keep it. And he taunts the social reformer: "What do you think of that, Proudhon?"°

Having seen how persistently Baudelaire's poetics tended toward what Hugo chose to do occasionally—*prendre à la prose un peu de son air familier*—we must now glance at the prose poem. The name looks like an oxymoron, but many poets would say—have said, like Cole- ridge—that the true distinction is not between those two words, but between poetry and science, meaning information, discourse about facts. If that is so, a poem can be written in either verse or prose. Long before Baudelaire, writers in every language used prose for elevated utterance, filled with imagery and showing in rhythm some of the characteristics of poetry. The absence of meter or rime, which constitute verse, make such a piece a prose poem.

Baudelaire's aim in his prose poems was to create "a poetic prose, musical but without rhythm or rime, flexible, yet jagged enough to adapt itself to the lyrical impulses of the soul, the wave-like motions of reverie, and the upheavals of conscience."° In these short pieces the poet treats again some of the themes of his verse. For example: "One must be always drunk, . . . so as not to feel the horrible burden of Time, which crushes your shoulders and bends your spine toward the Earth. . . ."° Others are sui generis—anecdotes exploit- ing the bizarre or using language several degrees below the level that his already colloquial lines would accommodate.

Whether all the fifty poems answer to his description is a question. Some of the prose has a perceptible rhythm; other parts of it are flat indeed and do not express any lyric impulse, reverie, or fit of conscience. The esthetics of the prose poem cannot, by its nature, be defined; it is a genre, not a form. At one extreme the poetic pulls toward incantation and at the other, the prosaic toward (let it be said with all due respect to Baudelaire) journalism. John Simon's admi-

---

Borrow from prose a little of its easy-going tone. ("A André Chénier," *Les Contemplations*, I, 5)

rable history and critique of the prose poem, examples of which are found in the late eighteenth century, leaves one with a sense of its possibilities and limitations—and its unavoidable touch of self-consciousness.° What remains clear is that Baudelaire's prose poems are, again, city pieces. The epilogue in verse he appended to them confirms the fact: the poet has climbed the hill from which he can see the whole town—"hospital, brothel, purgatory, hell, prison"—and he concludes: *Je t'aime, ô capitale infâme!*

Although there is one more great Parnassian—or demi-Parnassian—to deal with, Verlaine, I cannot leave Baudelaire, the prose poem, and the idea of specialized concentration in poetry without speaking of Poe. English and American critics have spent valuable thought wondering why the French poets of the last half of the nineteenth century were so enamored of the American. The critics consider him a negligible figure—inferior as poet and, in his fiction, at best a writer of popular entertainment. Yet after Baudelaire translated his tales and disseminated his ideas about poetry, Edgar Poe (as the French call him and as he was in fact known to his American contemporaries) became a great force in French poetics and literature generally. He was cited again and again as a far-sighted innovator in theory and practice; Mallarmé translated "The Raven" and wrote a sonnet for the Poe monument in Baltimore, a companion sonnet to the one for Baudelaire. It would be shameful, says Mallarmé, if "our thought" did not sculp

Un bas-relief
Dont la tombe de Poë éblouissante s'orne.

The key to the riddle of this hero-worship is simple: it lies in the fifteen pages of Poe's essay entitled "The Philosophy of Composition," which purports to tell how the author composed "The Raven." Because the critics think poorly of "The Raven" and do not believe Poe wrote it as he says he did, they neglect the "philosophy" stated in the opening pages. It consists of two main points: a poem can only be

---

I love you, O squalid capital!

A bas-relief / With which to decorate Poe's dazzling tomb. (*Le Tombeau d'Edgar Poë*). The reader may like to know why the French add a *tréma* (diaeresis) to Poe's name. It is to prevent the *oe* from being taken for a diphthong, which would entail the pronunciation *é* or *eu*.

short—long poems are made up of short bursts of true poetry tied together with prosy verse; and a true poem is not the product of inspiration but of careful, cold-blooded contriving.

These principles appealed immediately to the post-Romantic generation that wondered, among other things, what could be done after Lamartine, Musset, Hugo, and Vigny had manifestly exhausted every scheme and idea.° Poe insists on originality—it is, he says, a powerful means of catching the reader's interest. The explicit Cult of the New dates from those words, to which Poe adds in italics, an expression of surprise "that for centuries, no man, in verse, has ever done, or ever seemed to think of doing, an original thing." And less emphatically, almost casually, Poe states another principle: that a story gains immensely in artistry if it concentrates on a single episode and produces a single effect by taking care to use language adapted to the unique atmosphere.

In thus defining his invention, the short story (as against a tale that happens to be short), Poe was not only giving a formula equally applicable to the kind of poem he desiderated, but he was, indirectly, justifying the prose poem. A unified, "atmospheric" piece such as "The Fall of the House of Usher" may be seen as a prose poem. The tales Baudelaire translated were in their effect prose poems about a strange world. When, moreover, Poe's life became known—his struggles, his neglect by the public, his weaknesses and wretched death—the literary world in France added fellow-feeling to reasoned admiration.

That these distant followers of a congenial doctrine failed to assess as we do the worth of Poe's poetry is not to the point. It only proves once more how difficult poetic judgment is in the absence of native familiarity with the poet's language. But the adoption of that doctrine, like its emergence in America in Poe, a keen reader of European letters, shows that it answered a need of the times, not just an isolated quest.

No less important in the circumstances was the idea of Beauty. Poe considers it not a quality but an effect: the "intense and pure elevation of *soul*—*not* of intellect or of heart." Beauty is "the province of the poem," and its contemplation is the highest, purest pleasure. Poets have always wanted their works to be beautiful, but the beauty they attained was a mixed product, born of other concerns—panegyric, dramatic, erotic, satirical, elegiac, in a word, social. Now beauty had become a necessity for the human being as such, to *escape* the social, to live by contemplating it pure, to forget the concerns of intellect and heart, and receive from art the only pleasure left in a degraded world.

Poe's expression of these ideas paralleled and confirmed those gaining ground among artists in France and elsewhere; this alienation explains why these artists—the poets in particular—changed their aims and techniques. When Walter Pater said that all the arts tend toward the nature of music, he too was demanding significant beauty without articulate meaning; and when he prescribed for the good life the search for moments of intense contemplation in the presence of spiritual beauty, he was like Poe in describing what the world of artists and connoisseurs tried to practice in self-defense against vulgarity and "progress." In a word, aestheticism was the latest phase of culture; the word itself dates from 1858 and the critic who first applied it to a poem, disparagingly, explained: "it is music and picture, and nothing more."°

From these ideas to Verlaine is a short step. He figures as a Parnassian because he began publishing in the periodical that gave its name to the group. But he soon became a Decadent, and finally a Symbolist—or was taken by that school as their mentor. His *art poétique* begins:

> De la musique avant toute chose
> Et pour cela préfère l'impair.

So much for the means; now for the effect:

> Rien de plus cher que la chanson grise,
> Ou l'Indécis au Précis se joint.

These rules define poetic Impressionism; no hard edge and, as stated in the motto to this section, no eloquence—only suggestion. The *impair*, which means lines of odd-numbered feet, is to prevent "squareness," which is easily the result of alexandrines in serried ranks, especially those the Parnassians preferred to Hugo's endlessly varied swing. Verlaine used alexandrines too, but being primarily a lyricist, preferred short forms in short lines. In his early collection, *Fêtes Galantes*, inspired by Hugo's *La Fête chez Thérèse*, lines of eight and six syllables predominate and some of the "episodes" are in five and seven, his first trials of the *impair*.

What the Symbolists wanted and found in Verlaine was the fruit of

---

Music above all else / And to that end, prefer the uneven. / Nothing is dearer than the grayish song, / Where the Indefinite joins the Precise.

the merger he recommended between the precise and the indefinite. It spoke not directly but symbolically of an ideal realm transcending the present material world; and spoke of it, of course, musically. Note in passing that this ideal world now being imaged and fled to by sensitive artists was, if anything, even less clearly conceived than that of the Romanticists. They had a watered-down German philosophy, an early form, as one scholar has shown to be true for Lamartine, of twentieth-century Unanimism.° The Symbolists, although they took Mallarmé for a deep metaphysician, had little more than faith in art itself. Its possibility, its beauty, seemed to prove that not everything was useful and material.

Thus Mallarmé denounced procreation because it answered needs and multiplied solid objects. The universe, he decreed, exists only to produce The Book, meaning chiefly poetry. Accordingly, the facts or ideas that a poem seems to refer to are not actual or literal; if taken as such—*mis*taken—they yield no tenable sense, as for example in Verlaine's "Crépuscule du soir mystique":

Le Souvenir avec le Crépuscule
Rougeoie et tremble à l'ardent horizon
De l'Espérance en flamme qui recule
Et s'agrandit ainsi qu'une cloison
Mystérieuse où mainte floraison
—Dahlia, lys, tulipe et renoncule—
S'élance autour d'un treillis, et circule
Parmi la maladive exhalaison
De parfums lourds et chauds, dont le poison
—Dahlia, lys, tulipe et renoncule—
Noyant mes sens, mon âme et ma raison,
Mêle dans une immense pâmoison
Le Souvenir avec le Crépuscule.

This continuous sentence describes actions and relations that would defy any attempt at figuring out what does which and to

---

Remembrance reddens with the twilight / And trembles where the burning horizon / Of flaming Hope draws back / And grows like a mysterious partition / Where many a flowering / Of dahlia, lily, tulip, and crow-foot / Leaps around a trellis, and runs / Amid the sickly exhalation / Of hot, heavy odors, whose poison / —Dahlia, lily, tulip, and crow-foot— / Drowning my senses, my soul, and my reason / Mingles in a massive amorous faint / Remembrance with the twilight. (*Paysages tristes*, II)

whom. Try it and see at once the futility as well as the inappropriateness: the burning horizon of hope in flames draws back and grows like a mysterious partition where flowers leap around a trellis, etc. As a pure evocation, as word music playing on the tonic -zon, and as a kaleidoscope in which red and white stand out and diffuse a scent too heady for the twilit self made ecstatic by indefinite sensations of remembrance, it is beautifully calculated in all its effects. Verlaine's virtuosity in handling words and rhythms and in skirting definiteness is what made his work a model and earned his technique the name of vers libéré—not free, liberated.

Whether this new beauty elevated the soul as Poe wished is another question. Verlaine had phases of religious belief, but he was a shamelessly sensual being. Many of his poems depict overtly sexual scenes which doubtless helped to free literature from prudery. He had at command, by the way, more variety of suggestive detail than the perpetual breasts and thighs that poets since his day have found necessary to express their ultimate visions.

Verlaine, it is well known, also helped the young Rimbaud to make his way as a poet. A side effect of that association and of Verlaine's other wanderings is the injection of a new element into French poetry: acquaintance with the English language. Verlaine freely threw English words into some of his Romances sans paroles and gave them English titles: "Birds in the Night," "Green," "Child Wife." The title of Rimbaud's famous "Illuminations" is the English word that corresponds to the French enluminures, the colored initials with which medieval monks enlivened their copies of manuscripts. The author insisted that the word should denote colored engravings—pictures—not spiritual illumination.

It is further noteworthy that Mallarmé was a teacher of English; that Stuart Merrill and Vielé-Griffin (Symbolists also) were bilingual; and that Laforgue, who knew German well, married an Englishwoman. Paul Fort was explicit; he said he wanted his poetry to resemble the English, which he thought wonderfully "blurry" and "headlong," free of all conventions, as he believed Keats's work to be. Later, Claudel and St. John Perse resided in English-speaking lands and learned the language. Contact with another idiom marked a departure from the parochialism and chauvinism of French poets about their own tongue and incited them—or at least made it easy for them—to violate usage and syntax when seeking new effects. Nothing like this literary interlingualism had occurred for five hundred years.

Verlaine made vivid another aspect of poetry besides the foreign and the musical (his title *Romances sans paroles* meaning literally *Songs Without Words*). That other aspect is the poet's fate in modern society: he is unrecognized, tempted by drink and drugs, and as a result an outcast. Verlaine spent nearly four years in prison, first for shooting Rimbaud, then for nearly killing his own mother. The misfitness of poets had been noted before, but with Nerval, Baudelaire, and finally Verlaine and Rimbaud it virtually defined a social role. Verlaine gave it a name in a volume of short critical essays about the contemporaries he admired: *poètes maudits*.* They are accursed by their gift of poetry and by the unfeeling world into which they are born. Whether this is a necessary truth, the fact is that the Symbolist period saw a large number of its poets' lives end in dismal fashion, not only in France but elsewhere. Yeats was almost the sole robust and long-lived among them and he remarked with amazement about his stricken generation.

Despite his lyric genius and historical significance, Verlaine has been curiously treated by some of the best-known French anthologists. Gide gives him adequate space, but Thierry-Maulnier omits him and so do a couple of others. The critics and a number of poets (especially the Surrealists) relegate him to the class of minor figures as an elegant trifler; they seize upon the word *romance*, which means an unassuming parlor song, as his typical achievement.

This unfair estimate is due to a hidden tendency in modern judgments of poetry—indeed of art in general: Verlaine offers no emphatic message. The truth is that for all the talk of pure poetry and the contemplation of beauty, modern literature is read and valued to the degree that it criticizes modern life. Baudelaire's powerful appeal is his hatred of it; Mallarmé's rests on a proud, cryptic concealment of the alienated self and the allusion to a luminous elsewhere. And as more recent poets have bewailed the daily round and disgustedly surveyed the wasteland, they have turned to the colloquial for masochistic, denunciatory verisimilitude, a style that excludes "music" such as Verlaine wrought. Perhaps only Yevtushenko, as I related, is left to sing Verlaine's songs—in a Russian accent.

---

*These were: Tristan Corbière, Marceline Desbordes Valmore, Villiers de l'Isle Adam, Arthur Rimbaud, Stéphane Mallarmé, and Verlaine himself. The idea of malediction had been touched on by Baudelaire in the first poem of his book: "It is the Devil who pulls the strings that make us act."

The lack of faith in the future has developed
in the new poets an exclusive reliance on the
present, the immediate, and all art and liter-
ature reflects the feeling.
                              —André Gide (1947)

I have divided this essay into nine parts, perhaps with the Muses
vaguely in mind, for at times the thought occurred to me of giving
their names to one or another portion. To do it systematically, as
someone did for the books of Herodotus, was not possible. I would
have had to rename some of the sisters. Had I done so, this final
section would be called Anarchia. It would imply no confusion or
chaos, but only the strict meaning: absence of a common rule. The
poets of France and other Western nations go their own way, each
writing *comme bon lui semble*. Individuality and independence were
implied in the Romanticists' handling of the rules, even those that
they did not abrogate as Banville wished that Hugo had done—"all
but the golden bridle of rime."° By the end of their revolution that
bridle was thrown off too, along with any set structure for the line or
piece and any obedience to grammar and the dictionary. In that sense
only has anarchy meant violence.

It follows from this diverseness, this pluralism, that naming
anything like an *art poétique* or set of verse modes in modern French
poetry is not possible. Only individual poets show definable traits.
For the whole, enumeration is the best course; then purposes can be
grouped instead of men and given labels in abstract terms.

As for naming poets who are both representative and certifiably
"great," the attempt would be more than ever foolhardy. Look at
what has happened not just to Verlaine, but to Hugo and his peers, to
Nerval the Symbolist pioneer, to Boileau and Neo-classic starch,
and—heaven save!—to Ronsard and his satellites: for them, three
centuries of oblivion, then glorious exhumation. There is not, there
has never been, a consensus, except in school books. Teaching gen-
erates a vague sort of public opinion, for a time, but poets and critics
all the while make their passionate, incompatible, and self-assured
choices. The uncommitted reader is on his own.

From this point on, therefore, I must be content to describe aims
and attitudes as far as ascertainable, paying little attention to chronol-

ogy. The period, not "covered" but drawn on, goes from 1885 to the Second World War. It saw the appearance of dozens of "schools," manifestos, and little magazines, each promoting one or more poets and denouncing the rest. For this was the great age of artistic self-consciousness and theorizing.° The cult of the new required both. Earlier poets—Racine, Victor Hugo—knew what they were doing too and might write a preface justifying some aspect of the poetry in the book. But in recent times, the poet, before giving any samples, must clear the ground for them by an elaborate statement of intent. It reviews the current situation in poetry—always dire—appeals to a chosen precedent, and expounds the technical and philosophical rightness of the new departure.

Thus the public has been asked to lend an ear to Decadent, Symbolist, Paroxyst, Harmonist, Romanist, Scientific, Futurist, Dadaist, Surrealist, and other poetries, distinguishable or not, which together make up the body of work that Anglo-American readers for the first time in the history of French literature found accessible and enjoyable. Message and attitude proved congenial; and to appreciate the works as poetry, it was no longer necessary to know prosody or hear vowel sounds accurately. Other facilitating features will shortly become plain.

The first of the representative figures is Mallarmé. He too started as a Parnassian, much influenced by Baudelaire, as well as by Poe. Mallarmé was bent on being original—"astonishing," as Baudelaire had urged all poets to be. The early poems—some of the sonnets and the longer *Hérodiade* and *L'après-midi d'un faune*—are relatively "written in clear." Then come almost twenty years of struggle against sterility. Near the end of life, a new effort produced the poems called "hermetic," unintelligible without a key, the whole output being the slimmest of any French poet's of any note.

It is these last works that influenced several generations, not so much by inviting imitation as by showing what was in various respects permissible. For these few small poems and what the author said about them in print and in weekly talks with his devotees established an orthodoxy. First, the poem does not *tell;* it is an object. As such it can be taken to mean any number of things, all equally valid. The poet and critic Rémy de Gourmont said that "a tenable view of a Mallarmé poem will change on different evenings, like the clouds or the color of grass; the truth here and always is whatever our feeling of the moment decides."° Our late twentieth-century excitement over the idea (also French) that there is no such thing as a literary text, only a reader's relation to shifty marks on paper, is obviously an idea *réchauffé*'d almost a century after its emergence. In our century also this preference for variable meanings, for the ambiguous that creates the optional—all avenues of freedom—was accompanied by the reacceptance of myth as a form of true knowledge, an opinion fed and strengthened by the publication of Fraser's *Golden Bough.*

Gourmont's view goes with yet another belief: "music" and unconscious suggestion are superior to articulate statement. In another essay, the critic contradicts Romain Rolland (and factual truth) and asserts that in French poetry accent falls on sounds, not on sense.° What this dictum really supports is the root principle of Symbolism: the inadequacy of language to pinning down thought. The whole modern movement in literature is grounded on dissatisfaction with words. Besides, Baudelaire's hatred of the newspaper was shared by every writer who aimed at "art." Common speech, the cliché, political and religious rhetoric were despised like the machine-made things they resembled. Hence the desire to remake grammar, syntax, and vocabulary into something new and strange and fit for poetry. So here at least *sunt tamen inter se communia sacra poetis.** Mallarmé coined the slogan of this crusade in a line of the Poe sonnet:

> Donner un sens plus pur aux mots de la tribu

The contradiction between a purer meaning and one that does and should vary for each reader does not matter; it is inevitable, since the Mallarmean poet wants to be at once exact and ambiguous. But where does he find, or how does he make, that purer meaning which shall cleanse the vocabulary of its journalistic filth? A scholar named Charles Chassé discovered the answer and thereby cast a new light on Mallarmé's method. He found that the poet went to the great Littré dictionary, the equivalent of the *OED,* and sought the pure meanings among the etymologies.° Thus, in the first line of the Poe sonnet for

---

Give a purer meaning to the words of the tribe.
Mallarmé translated his poem into English for the benefit of Sarah Whitman, Poe's love. There are a couple of mistakes in English, including the curious rendering of this sixth line as: "To give *too pure* a meaning. . . ." (Italics added)

*Yet there is a common tie among poets. (Ovid, *Epistolae* II, 10)

the word *grief*, which in modern French means complaint or griev-
ance, Mallarmé gives in his English version the meaning "struggle."
The link is the etymology *gravis*, burden, which by a further turn
based on Latin usage denotes "effort." Other examples are: *veuf* used
for "empty" instead of "widowed"; *nubile* for "cloudy" instead of
marriageable; *encombre* for "accident" instead of "obstruction"; *linceul*
for "(bed)sheet" instead of "shroud." The purification seems to con-
sist in removing connotations, neutralizing the bias or force acquired
in use.

The result of this search for roots makes of the hermetic poem
something other than it has seemed: it must now be seen as a
translation from a definite, unambiguous text into one that is many-
faceted by virtue of meanings borrowed from the past and substi-
tuted as in a code for the plain originals. An analogy would be: a
familiar folk tune harmonized and orchestrated by Richard Strauss;
only by an effort could one discover the contour of the popular
utterance.

Mallarmé concealed his procedure as he had every right to do, but
once or twice he made puzzling remarks about it. When someone
asked him to interpret a certain poem, he answered: "Work it out. In
the end, you'll find pornography; that will be your reward." Perhaps
the reply was meant for a joke. But the frequent erotic descriptions
that appear in the hermetic works when deciphered make it more
likely that he was serious.

Nor was etymology his only veiling device. He had a private
mythology, in which the daily rising of the sun was a miracle he
called the "supreme game." It figures in the well-known:

> Une dentelle s'abolit
> Dans le doute du Jeu suprême
> A n'entr'ouvrir comme un blasphème
> Qu'absence éternelle de lit.

The bed in the last line stands for procreation, which Mallarmé,
despite his eroticism, made a symbol of the regrettable habit of
producing human beings. He shared Schopenhauer's view that
sexuality imposes the curse of desire upon the unborn. Rather, the
poet says he would have preferred gestation inside a lute (*mandore*); it

---

A piece of lace destroys itself / In the uncertainty of the Supreme Game /
To open up like blasphemy / Only the eternal absence of a bed.

would signify: to come forth, like music, from a hollow, that is, the void.

Between transposable words and mythic symbols, then, Mallarmé's sonnets and other poems make definite statements, like the works of previous poets. His artistry resides in the usual features of syllable count and rime—rich rime. In these matters Mallarmé remained perfectly regular. Nor can he be accused of excessive inversion, because his syntax rather splits than inverts. He was in fact a strict Parnassian, much more staid than Verlaine (whom he admired), though like him desirous of musicality. On this point there is a sharp difference between the plain works and the hermetic; the latter can hardly be called either word magic or word music. Their syntax being dislocated, one must collect the sentence from separate fragments as in a Latin ode, and since these fragments have only partial meaning, the flow of even a short line is interrupted. For instance:

> A la nue accablante tu
> Basse de basalte et de laves
> A même les échos esclaves
> Par une trompe sans vertu
>
> Quel sépulcral naufrage (tu
> Le sais, écume, mais y baves)
> Suprême une entre les épaves
> Abolit le mât dévêtu. . . .

Only line two in the first quatrain and three in the second have anything approaching harmony in their enunciation; and the first of these is dimmed by a puzzle at the outset: where to attach *basse?* It looks like the feminine of *bas* (low) which might modify *nue* (cloud) in line 1. But no, it is a technical term of navigation unknown to the most educated readers: a reef never fully exposed regardless of tides. (Littré's dictionary at work again.)

The meaning in clear of this octet begins in the second stanza, with the address to Foam [*écume*]: You who have dribbled over the shipwreck know how many deaths (*quel sépulcral*) it caused, only you,

------

To the oppressive cloud kept quiet / Submerged reef of basalt and lava / Even the enslaved echoes / By a trump without virtue / What a sepulcral shipwreck thou / Knowest, foam, but slobbering over it / Supreme among the flotsam / Destroyed the undressed mast. . . . (*Plusieurs sonnets*)

after it broke the mast, stripped of its sail, supreme among the pieces
of wreckage, because the horror of it has been concealed (*tu*) from the
oppressive clouds as black over the sea as a reef of basalt and lava, by
the failure of the ship's siren (*trompe*). Six lines more merely add detail
to this compacted view of a disaster at sea.

The very traps set by Mallarmé for the hasty reader interfere with
such harmony as he may have planned. That the *tu* in the first line
turns out to be the past participle of *taire* (keep quiet), instead of *tu*
(thou), appears solely from the fact that it rimes with the *tu* in line 5;
that is, one must have faith in the poet's obedience to the rule that a
word should not rime with itself. Again, *à même* is an idiom meaning
"immediately next to," but here it is used as if the *à* did not exist, and
the sense is plain "even." Similarly, *laves* has an *s* only to match
esclaves, though one would normally make the link *tu . . . laves*
(thou washest), it being unlikely that "lava" should be used in the
plural.

This wilful chopping up of melody confirms what I suggested in an
earlier section about the role of meaning in producing musicality.
When the sense and the sound do not go together in subtle parallel for
some distance, that pleasure is denied. The later Mallarmé denies it,
often at every line—and not by their shortness. One has only to
compare Verlaine, still musical at his shortest:

> Dans l'interminable
> Ennui de la plaine
> La neige incertaine
> Luit comme du sable.

Music was valued because it is inexplicit. But applied to poetry
that is a mere notion. How did the art of music itself come into the
poets' ken, if indeed it did? The answer could never be guessed.
Suddenly, in the mid-1880s, nearly all French men of letters fell into
a frenzy of devotion toward one musician—Wagner. Most of these
men and women had not been concert goers; they were not by gift or
study musicians; what they wrote in the *Revue Wagnérienne* that they
began to publish makes this fact clear. But they found in their idol so
many things to comfort or justify their souls that they could not let
him alone. Here was a poet-musician whose operas dealt no longer
with human drama but with a mythic world full of symbols. His

---

In the endless / Boredom of the plain / The uncertain snow / Shines like
sand. (*Ariettes Oubliées, VIII*)

work, moreover, was not haphazard inspiration but based on theory, contrived according to a system like mosaic, one which incidentally taught the listener by repetition to enjoy what he heard. And Wagner typified the artist, too, because he had been long resisted by the philistines. But a king had come to his rescue and made him wealthy and powerful. All artists must applaud, and when they did not understand they must study. The one musical mind among them, Romain Rolland, declared that when the music baffled him he did not lose faith, because the system was there to resolve the doubts. °

Mallarmé's own system for making mosaics out of disguised phrases—a kind of return to the circumlocutions of Delille—had still more momentous consequences. The willingness of his contemporaries to work out or day-dream in the presence of the contrived puzzles established the right of literature to be not merely difficult but uncommunicative. The obscurities in Browning that led to societies all over England for unraveling his thought were not in the same class, because Browning intended a meaning and could be, as it were, called to account. Mallarmé, whatever he intended, gave license to the use of entirely private imagery, solipsism confronting public opinion.

But the effect was not one-sided. This new art liberated the reader as well as the poet, and in so doing satisfied a general feeling of fatigue. Clear meaning had become a bore. In the fine arts, subjects became taboo; painting and sculpture were to be forms only; they "evoked," and the beholder could make up his own interpretation of the patterns he saw or thought he saw, just as in Mallarmé.

On the creator's side, it restored something of his power and glory to the accursed artist. He might be in the gutter or the alcoholic ward, but he was no longer a purveyor of goods for public consumption. Not that he had felt like one in the Romanticist era of the poet-seer; but his role then still implied a relation between the genius and the people. Now the bond had snapped. True, the poet might still have worldly ambitions, as Mallarmé evidently had when he took pains to promote his writings and condescended to write florid advertising for cosmetics, not out of need. But with the growing cult of art the wretched, unrewarded poet took on the likeness of a saint.

This change coincided with another, or possibly precipitated it: literature began to be studied, not just read. From Mallarmé to the present a vast academic enterprise turns out both tracts and glosses on the written word almost as soon as it appears, and it deals by preference with the enigmatic. Debate still rages over the forty-odd hermetic poems of Mallarmé, and by the Symbolist definition of art there cannot be an end. Eager for problems, the academic microscope has been lowered on authors of all periods, and it makes out things that are not there or not worth attention—for instance, where the accent should fall on the word *majestueusement*, which is the second half of a line by Vigny. Is that half-line "organized"? Yes, all is well, because in reading a "countertonic" accent is supplied "spontaneously" at the fourth syllable.° There is such a thing as killing by dissection—killing pleasure at any rate, and in effect making literature a means instead of an end. But one should not complain too loudly, because without the grindings of the academic mill it is a question whether most of "our major poets" and our major other things would continue to be heard of.

After Mallarmé, the next emancipation came from Verlaine's young protégé, Arthur Rimbaud. A precocious youth, he produced all his works in five years, giving up poetry at the age of twenty. His lycée teacher, Georges Izambard, encouraged his first efforts, which Rimbaud himself described in a fragment as "the writings of a young, quite young man, whose life developed here and there, without a mother or a country, indifferent to all knowledge, running away from every moral force, like many another pitiable young man."°

From his earliest poems, though using all the devices of Romanticist versification, Rimbaud gave hints of his characteristic mode of thought: it is in essence free association in a mind possessed by violent emotions—love of the ideal and resentment of his own lot. Toward others, he swings between pity and contempt. It is the Baudelaire mixture as before, but increased in voltage by extraordinary leaps of thought. Rimbaud's view of himself as "indifferent to all knowledge" should be read with the stress on indifferent; his knowledge of words and facts is enormous, but what he knows yields only hatred of the world.

In verse, his comprehensive statement is *Bateau ivre*—Drunken boat. The ship reports its wanderings in a way that recalls Vigny's floating flask, but without any implied "moral force":

> Mais, vrai, j'ai trop pleuré. Les aubes sont navrantes
> Toute lune est atroce et tout soleil amer.
> L'âcre amour m'a gonflé de vapeurs enivrantes
> Oh! que ma quille éclate! Oh! que j'aille à la mer!

───────────

But really, I have wept too long. Dawns are too saddeningly / Every moon is cruel and every sun bitter, / Sour love had made me swell with intoxicating vapors. / Oh, let my hull explode! Oh, let me go to sea! /

Si je désire une eau d'Europe, c'est la flache
Noire et froide où vers le crépuscule embaumé
Un enfant accroupi, plein de tristesse, lâche
Un bateau frêle comme un papillon de mai.

Je ne puis plus, baigné de vos langueurs, ô lames,
Enlever leur sillage aux porteurs de cotons,
Ni traverser l'orgueil des drapeaux et des flammes,
Ni nager sous les yeux horribles des pontons!

This and other poems in different meters show the utmost regularity; the rimes are rich, the lines mostly self-contained—few enjambments or none; and the music is in peaceful contrast with the warring images: an earlier stanza in *Bateau ivre* speaks of its handsome pine-wood keel "stained with wine and vomitings," the sea serpents it encounters are "eaten up by bedbugs." The pervasive horror of life makes tenderness or beauty collapse again and again into cruelty and sordor—a device for which the Romanticists used to be severely blamed. But in Rimbaud's age of esthetic specialization, the insistent effect creates a new reality: there *is* no beauty or tenderness except in the poet's soul. Rimbaud's ardent disciple Claudel makes the point by quoting: "The true life is missing. We are not in the world," and in this awareness Claudel feels the spur to "recovering our primitive state." One must not flee this world, but find the "true life" through faith in God.

That is one interpretation of Rimbaud by a fellow poet who "took him at his word and trusted him."° The same conclusion could be drawn from Baudelaire's religious longings and denunciation of the world. But both poets could also be taken as "Abolitionists"—not a school, but a name I choose to fit many of the writers of the latter days of the nineteenth century—Lautréamont, Laurent Tailhade, Tristan Corbière, Aristide Bruant, Alfred Jarry—with Rimbaud their model. For in saying that by his words and his "disordering of the senses," he wanted to "change life, create new worlds, new flesh, and new languages," he implied the destruction of the world we know. As early as 1871, after the uprising and massacre of the Paris Commune, Rimbaud wrote a poem that shouts: "Europe, Asia, America, per-

---

If I long for any of the waters of Europe, it is some water hole / Cold and black, where in the scented dusk / A squatting child, full of sadness, launches / A boat as frail as a May butterfly. / I cannot, bathed in your languor, O waves, / Erase the cotton freighters' wake / Nor cross the pride of flags and pennants / Nor swim beneath the pontoons' dreadful eyes.

ish!" Begin by "overthrowing all order." But at the end the poet still despairs: he himself is still around.° It was left to Jarry, the author of the play *Ubu roi*, to give the ultimate recipe: "We will bring everything down in ruins, and then we will destroy the ruins."

The Abolitionists introduced insult as a new element in polite literature. Tailhade's *Au Pays du Mufle* (In the Country of the Snouts) calls by that name the "ignominious middle class," and for a collection of poems subtitled "To Displease the Many," he takes as motto another poet's dictum, "The bourgeois must be pissed upon." Tailhade's verses on this theme are expertly put together, full of archaic and learned words interspersed with vicious personalities.°

The attack on the bourgeois was not new: Gautier in his famous preface to *Mlle de Maupin* in 1834 had delineated the philistine once for all and proclaimed that art was for art's sake. But the Abolitionist venom two generations later had the added grievance that the hateful world they rejected had been made such by bourgeois enterprise and greed. The artist's poverty that Rimbaud "execrated" was part and parcel of what the middle class called progress. His prose poem "Democracy" denounces "monstrous military or industrial exploitation" and ends: "Our philosophy will be fierce; ignoramuses in science, libertines in comfort; to hell with the world as it goes. Forward, march!" Nerval at mid-century had inveighed against money, which he saw as the emblem of power, replacing birth and breeding. After him, writers and intellectuals—some of them probably thinking of Wagner—imagined a time when cultivated dukes had made it a habit to say: "My dear poet, what can I do for you? You have but to ask"—and said this to the *right* poets. That time never existed, but its mirage justified the insults and the spreading *ressentiment*.

The works of Rimbaud that express this animus are the prose poems in Part II of *Les Illuminations* and those in *Une Saison en Enfer*. Both collections contain quasi metaphysical, social, and autobiographical statements from which may be deduced an unrelieved nihilism, and with equal plausibility a call to the love of God. The form of these prose pieces—two of them entitled "Delirium"—is itself an invitation to giving up the rational mind: logic is worthless, pure deception. In the piece called *Alchimie du Verbe* (Alchemy of and through Words), the account of his "madnesses" is more convincing than the stated outcome, which is: the poet, being purged, is now "able to salute Beauty."

Before that consummation, the poem mirrors the unreality of what is: "It was at first a plan of study: I wrote silences, nights, I noted the inexpressible, I pinned down dizziness. . . . Weeping, I used to see gold—and could not drink. . . . The old poetic tricks had a fair part in my alchemy through words. I accustomed myself to plain hallucination. I readily saw a mosque where stood a factory, a school of drummers made up of angels . . . a drawing room at the bottom of a lake. . . . I began to find the disorder of my mind holy. Oh, the little fly made drunk by the urinal at the inn, very fond of borage, and which one ray of the sun dissolves . . . I became a fabulous opera: . . . action is not life but a means of spoiling some force, an irritation. Morality is the weakness of the brain." And in the next poem: "Having found two cents' worth of reason—it goes by so quickly!—I see that my ailments come from not having seen soon enough that we are in the West. My two cents' worth are over! The mind is Authority, it insists that I be in the West. One would have to shut it up to end up where I wanted."

There, surely, was a transmutation (alchemy) of the daily world sufficient to inspire many kinds of revolt and many kinds of poems, in prose or some other form. The principle of discontinuity was established for good, and with Mallarmé's doctrine of private imagery for multiple meanings, the two components of modern poetry were available to anyone who wanted to embroider the theme of Abolition.

After 1900 came the violent manifestos of Marinetti and his Futurist followers, which taught the same lesson in detail. Marinetti has been unjustly ignored—for political reasons: he later became a Fascist—but (writing in French and also quoting Poe as inspirer) he helped dissolve the grammatical and the logical: get rid of adjectives and adverbs; always make nouns double—"man-torpedo, woman-harbor, crowd-ground-swell, door-faucet"; use no punctuation; "create the maximum disorder." Don't be "afraid of the ugly" and "change spelling ad lib for expressiveness."° All this in 1912. Later agents of disruption seem like repeaters: *Dada détruit et se borne à cela* dates from 1919, and Breton's *Manifeste du Surréalisme* in 1924 uses many words to say that "Language has been given to man to be used surrealistically," which is: let the words come by association, automatically—"it is not my business to favor some at the expense of others." It appears from Breton's long list of great writers that when they wrote well they followed or yielded to this precept: "Hugo is a Surrealist when he is not a dope."°

Dadaism destroys and is content to do no more.

With Mallarmé's broken syntax in mind and the discontinuous "logic" of Rimbaud's prose poem, one must glance back for a moment at the kindred developments in French prose, for it too "wanted art." This lack exasperated the Goncourt brothers, joint authors of novels and histories, who shared the contemporary loathing for the press and its style. Rimbaud had said of *Les Misérables* that it was a great poem because its prose was unlike any other. Flaubert was struggling against his provincial upbringing to clear *his* prose of vulgarity while making harmony of it by excluding repetition and rhetoric. The Goncourts took the plunge and tried systematically to remake the stuff and structure of the medium itself. They made up hundreds of new words and turns of phrase, digging up archaic terms and tacking on modern endings, "misusing" prepositions, piling up adjectives *before* the noun, English-fashion, and abandoning the short, sober sentence—the Voltairian model—in favor of sinuous groups of clauses "molded on psychological reality."° This they called *"prose d'art"*; the rest was just prose. But the story does not end here. It resumes when the evolution of French poetry made the distinction between the two media less and less perceptible, more and more arbitrary, until the novel itself adopted the anti-logical features of poetry.

Obviously in the 1880s all serious writers had but one aim: to be evocative. Sound-before-meaning was the only art that could shield the beholder from the intolerable sight of the world. And the world included the ideas and sentiments that literature itself had diffused and thus rendered loathsome. But rejecting is easier than getting rid of. Abolition is not a plan but a cause, which is why the cry has had to be raised so often over the years—more than half a century. The public may even applaud; but its old ways persist, and the upshot is that artists continue to feel imprisoned and give vent to another demand—freedom.

In the welter of theories launched in France from the Symbolist decade to the first postwar period, such was the recurrent desire and promise. Freedom is the word that comes again and again before or after the call for "invention," the relentless search for the new. Invention evidently did not come of its own accord and poets thought it would be there for the plucking if only they could be free. From what? Apparently from the shackles of traditional versification.

It seems incredible that after Hugo, Mallarmé, Verlaine, and the prose poem the prison door should have been found locked. Yet so it was. Verlaine had preached and practiced the *vers libéré*—lines in which the rules about cesura, hiatus, rime, and mute *e* were treated cavalierly; "liberated" meant no more than that. Verse was out on parole, so to speak, it was not yet free. When the next step was taken, it was to be the *vers* [entirely] *libre*, chronologically the third application of the phrase, this time meaning: no list of rules. But still the call to freedom kept sounding, as I have said; the fact being that every system or no-system hardens into habits and formulas that the next comers feel as constraints.

What are the characteristics of this ultimate *vers libre?* The main one is *le rythme* or rhythmical unit. This unit could be of any length or form; it grew out of the poet's impulse as he conceived his subject and it would differ from poet to poet and from line to line within a poem. With it, each creator could use rime or assonance or neither. No set stanzas, no pattern made visible by repetition need occur; the form of the poem would be a result instead of a preselection. The last two pieces in Rimbaud's *Illuminations* that Verlaine published in 1886 date back to 1872 or '73 and are the first modern *vers libres* on record. °
The last stanza of the second reads:

> Aux accidents atmosphériques les plus surprenants,
> Un couple de jeunesse s'isole sur l'arche;
> Est-ce ancienne sauvagerie qu'on pardonne?—
> Et chante et se poste.

Presumably, each line is one of those *rythmes* called forth by the image or the make-up of the words, but the net effect is that of prose with occasional cadences barely perceptible. The first line sounds like seven iambuses; the next could pass for an alexandrine; the third is another, provided the mute *e*'s are given their due; and the last is half an alexandrine, with yet another mute ending at the cesura. Except for the break at each end of line, there is no intrinsic difference between this poem in *vers libres* and the prose poem:

"Des fleurs magiques bourdonnaient. Les talus le berçaient.

To the most surprising atmospheric accidents, / A youthful couple go to be alone on the arch; / Is it an ancient, wild shyness one forgives? / —And sings and takes its stand.

Magic flowers were buzzing. / Embankments cradled him. /

Des bêtes d'une élégance fabuleuse circulaient. Les nuages s'amass-
aient sur la haute mer faite d'une éternité de chaudes larmes."

Certainly, the conception and imagery in each poem offer no ground
for preferring one form to the other. The second could also be printed
in four lines instead of straight on.

A curious question has arisen for the historian: did Walt Whit-
man's brand of free verse, written long before the French made up the
term and the scheme, play a part in this phase of their versification?
After reading a careful survey based on the testimony of a good
number of poets who outlived the century, I do not believe in any
such influence.° And I can add a small scrap of evidence: in my copy,
inherited from my father, of the first translation of *Leaves of Grass* by
León Bazalgette in 1908, the original advertising flyer is preserved.
On it several of the quotations from reviews say in effect: "If ever
Walt Whitman is to become known and appreciated in France, these
volumes [including a biography] will be the means." So twenty years
after Rimbaud, *Leaves of Grass* was still a novelty.

The excitement over *vers libre* belongs to the late 1880s. It was then
that Vielé-Griffin used as a motto on his volume of poems: *Le vers est
libre* and offered a theory of its construction; it was then that Marie
Krysinska claimed to be the originator of the form; it was then that
Laforgue, Dujardin, Henri de Régnier, Moréas, Gustave Kahn, and
others began to fill the little magazines with *vers libres*. The interested
reader would derive profit and enjoyment from Amy Lowell's solid
study of *Six French Poets* of the *vers libre* school. It gives copious
extracts with translations, biographical details, and good criticism
from the point of view of an Imagist poet. Only an occasional
misjudgment need be guarded against, as when it is said that Mal-
larmé made the alexandrine "undulating and more tuneful"—the
exact opposite of the truth.°

The theorists of *vers libre*, notably Gustave Kahn, recommended
assonance as a way of indicating pattern without resorting to the
emphatic, regularizing stroke of rime. Alliteration, too, could be
used to make sure of proselessness; and an occasional internal rime
could be tolerated if it came without effort; its music would be
"natural." When rime was used, it was rime by sound only; the silent

---

Animals fabulously elegant went about. / Clouds were massing on the
high seas made of an eternity of tears. (Division by slashes added.)

letters formerly required were ignored. A few lines from Laforgue illustrate the mixture of the devices:

> La lune se lève
> O route en grand rêve!
> On a dépassé les filatures, les scieries,
> Plus que les bornes kilométriques,
> Des petits nuages de confiserie,
> Cependant qu'un fin croissant de lune se lève
> O route de rêve, o nulle musique.

The two twelve-syllable lines (three and six) may be accidental, but whereas *lève* and *rêve* are standard rimes, and *kilométriques* and *musique* also, except for matching a plural with a singular, *scieries* and *confiserie* play with double assonance in *i* and combine it with *rie* to form the kind of rime the Middle Ages called leonine.°

Vers libre is still being used today, but it is remarkable that in spite of the incessant demand for freedom, the outstanding French poets of the last hundred years have either abandoned *vers libre* after starting out with it, or have switched between free and measured verse in successive poems, or have fashioned combinations of the two in one work, not ever giving up the alexandrine or its convenient half line.

The vocabulary, of course, has been totally free, ranging from the most traditional poetic diction to slang and obscenity and finding its ultimate liberation in automatic writing and in aleatory (random) arrangement. The Dadaist poem, according to Tristan Tzara, is made by taking a newspaper (shades of Baudelaire!), cutting up a column into single words, putting the scraps in a bag, shaking it "gently" and, taking out one word at a time, copying them "conscientiously"—*le poème vous ressemblera.*"°

Few of these hand-made works are to be found in anthologies or critical surveys. But the regular, the irregular, the colloquial, the prose poem, and intermediate forms alluding at will to the past have kept on appearing since Rimbaud and Laforgue began to play with

---

The moon is rising / Oh, road wrapped in dream / We've gone beyond the textile mills, the lumber mills, / Nothing but the kilometer markers, / Small clouds as if from a candy shop, / While a slim crescent moon is rising, / Oh, dream road, oh, worthless music. ("Solo de lune")

The poem will sound like you.

the inherited materials. Here is part of Laforgue's "The Moon's Complaint in the Provinces"; except for the liberties taken with the visual riming, it might have been written by Musset, who also was a moon-gazer:

> Ah! la belle pleine lune,
> Grosse comme une fortune!
>
> La retraite sonne au loin,
> Un passant, monsieur l'adjoint; . . .
>
> Calme lune, quel exil!
> Faut-il dire: ainsi soit-il?. . . .
>
> Lune, o dilettante lune
> A tous les climats commune . . . .
>
> Et la lune a, bonne vieille,
> Du coton dans les oreilles.

Out of the prose poem and the flexible *vers libre* came yet another form, for which the name *verset*, borrowed from its designation of the verses of the Bible, denotes the poems of Claudel and others, including St. John Perse. The genre consists of long declarative sentences having the amplitude of sound and the solemnity of feeling of their counterparts in scripture. Here is Claudel giving his *art poétique* in the form he devised:

> O mon âme! le poème n'est point fait de ces lettres
> que je plante comme des clous, mais du blanc qui
> reste sur le papier.
>
> O mon âme, il ne faut concerter aucun plan, ô mon
> âme sauvage, il nous faut tenir libres et prêts,
> Comme les immenses bandes fragiles d'hirondelles
> quand sans voix retentit l'appel automnal!
>
> O mon âme impatiente, pareille à l'aigle sans art!
> comment ferions-nous pour ajuster aucun vers? à

Ah, the fair full moon / Large as great wealth! / Far off the bugle plays taps, / A passer-by, the deputy mayor . . . . / Peaceful moon, wretched exile! / Should one say "so be it"? / Moon, oh dilettante moon / The same in all climes . . . / And the moon, good old crone, / Has cotton in her ears.

l'aigle qui ne sait pas faire son nid même?
Que mon vers ne soit rien d'esclave! . . .

The cry for freedom in these lines is coupled with the summons to spontaneity. The length of line is not predetermined, there is no rime or metrical pattern, *le rythme* asserts itself as idea and image dictate; incantation is level with evocation. But in spite of the poet's "wild soul" and resolve not to let his verse be enslaved, he ends a few lines later by expressing confidence that the "moderating" Muses will not abandon him.

The *verset* in Claudel and Perse seeks the needed strangeness of poetry by what has been called "translation style," the deliberate avoidance of the idiomatic. This device goes back to Mallarmé, whose lines often transliterate English turns of phrase. But these later poets cling to naturalness as well by keeping to the normal syntax.

Out of the same religious fervor as Claudel's, an elaboration of free verse into a similar method was made by Péguy, who heightened the incantatory effect by tireless though modified repetition:

Ainsi l'enfant dormait dans son premier sommeil,
Ainsi l'enfant dormait dans son premier berceau,
Ainsi l'enfant dormait dans son premier repos,
Ainsi l'enfant dormait dans son premier bercail.

and so on for seven lines more that show but trifling changes in the first six words of each line. And the next idea occupies a similar group of lines with alternative endings. Throughout, approximate rimes are used: above, *sommeil* and *bercail* are neither rimes nor assonances, but the y(*e*) sound is in both.

This system was not imitated, but its bearing deserves attention. Péguy's poetry and prose alike show the modern dissatisfaction,

---

Oh my soul! a poem is not made with these letters that I drive in like nails, but with the white space left on the paper. / Oh my soul, one must not devise any plan; oh my wild soul, we must keep ourselves free and ready, / Like the great frail flocks of swallows when the voiceless call of autumn resounds! / Oh my impatient soul, akin to the artless eagle! How could we possibly tailor a verse? to the eagle who does not even know how to make his own nest? / Let my verse be in no way a slave! ("Les Muses," *Cinq grandes odes*)

Thus did the child sleep in his first slumber / . . . . first cradle / . . . first rest / . . . first sheep-fold. / (*Eve*)

restlessness, impatience with language itself. It seems at once inade-
quate and used up, doubly inadequate because used up: in poetry it
had been fully exploited by the Romanticists and in prose by the
high-grade literature of the merely talented. Words of every species
were too familiar. Péguy says apropos of a line he admires in a poem
by Hugo: "Which proves that one line is always greater than several.
As also one word is greater than several. And so I cannot stand people
who set down several words."°

The last dictum is amusing when one thinks of Péguy's poetry *or*
prose. Here is a sample of the latter: "The more the gift of verse came
to him, welled up in him, of profound verse, of—so to speak—deaf-
and-blind verse, verse with unlimited resonance, with infinitely
profound resonance, the more was order lacking, the inner order, the
deep organism, the organic structure, the organization of the organic,
the order of an organization, the organization of the tragic, a deeper
order."° One is tempted to agree here that one word would be greater
than several, and also to murmur that organization seems to be
missing.

But Péguy's inconsistency does not matter when we find him at
work among the deliberate language-mongers, the stutterers for art's
sake, such as Gertrude Stein and Gerard Manley Hopkins. The one
repeats like Péguy to squeeze all possible meaning out into the open;
the other moves forward by a blend of alliteration and punning that is
also intended to thicken the sense as ordinary words, he felt, were
unable to do.*

This struggle was rooted in new perceptions. Rimbaud was appar-
ently gifted with synesthesia—seeing colors when hearing sounds
(like the composer Scriabin) and toyed with the idea of a poetry that
would reach all the senses. The "art prose" of the Goncourts was
intended to do just that, and the incredible words throughout the
prose of the Symbolists or the verse of Tailhade, which sound
ridiculous today, were earnest attempts at a sort of total "redecora-
tion" of human speech—and a reconstruction too. Mallarmé, at the

---

*Gertrude Stein gives up more than organization: "Now think carefully. A sentence
may be what they said. It may not be what they thank for. It may be what they will in have.
He does not like have in a sentence. If a sentence is careful. A sentence is carefully made a
sentence is carefully cared to for her sake. Sentences made slowly. With them with whom.
In a minute sentences made slowly. Made slowly." (*How to Write*, Paris, 1931, p. 211)

very end, found his cryptograms insufficient by themselves and composed a poster-like poem, *Jamais un coup de dé n'abolira le hasard*, in which blank spaces and lines differentiated by typography recreate the poetic "object" in its true relations, the ones that grammar fails to create.

From this work, anti-linear and not to be "read" but grasped, have come all the ventures into "multiplicity," through visual, typographic means, from Simultanism, Futurism, the choric poem, and polyphonic prose to concrete poetry. By that time, the influence of the despised outer world was not denied. We know from a diary of 1913 kept by the excellent poet Paul Eluard that the right image for his view of the poem is "the cinema film, where a series of pictures taken from the component parts of an action . . . can be joined into a flowing resemblance to human movement. . . . I write poetry as a series of sense images which coalesce at the end of several lines into a coherent unit."° The first of three quatrains entitled "Poissons" reads:

> Les poissons, les nageurs, les bateaux
> Transforment l'eau.
> L'eau est douce et ne bouge
> Que pour ce qui la touche.

Eluard, though later and temporarily a Surrealist, was content with the cumulative effect of images to be read one after the other. The Simultanists, like Mallarmé, wanted them taken in all at once. The compromise between the two was Joyce's telescoped words in *Finnegans Wake*, which partly defy the convention of one idea at a time. These innovations lie outside my purview—there is nothing to say about versification in their make-up. But their occurrence is indicative of that other purpose I mentioned: while poetry was straining to become music, prose narrative—the novel—was straining to be poetry. I suggested that the short story as defined by Poe was potentially a prose poem; the next step was to inject poetic

---

"Never will a throw of dice eliminate Chance."

The fish, the swimmers, the boats / Transform the waters. / Water is gentle and does not stir / Except for what touches it. ("Poissons," *Les Animaux et leurs Hommes Les Hommes et leurs Animaux*)

spontaneity and strangeness into story-telling. This was what a very young poet, Dujardin, did in *Les lauriers sont coupés* with his invention of the "interior monologue." He defined it as a means of "expressing the most intimate thoughts, those closest to the Unconscious . . . [the] speech that precedes logical thought." This, he added, necessarily entails "reducing statements to a syntactical minimum."°

Dujardin's small book, published in 1887, had no success in his day, but Joyce read it in 1901 and later acknowledged that it was the source of his inner soliloquies in *Ulysses*. For this first decade of the new century was the time when Pound and Eliot, Apollinaire, Marinetti, Johannes Schlaf and Richard Dehmel, F.S. Flint, Stefan Zweig, Oscar Milosz, Richard Aldington, and other foreigners flocked to Paris and borrowed or adapted forms and styles from the many-sided offering. (A little later, Robert Bridges tried out syllabic verse in English, and he has had followers in the United States.) That the Paris novelties were "the last word" may be taken in two senses: it marked the end of a long tradition; the cult of the new, like all progress, exhausts the natural resources. At the same time, it was a new primitivism, the poet in despair acting as if present at the birth of language.

This odd combination appears again in the new respect paid, in England, to nonsense verse. Edward Lear and Lewis Carroll were in fact the first coiners of "portmanteau" words, well before Joyce; and the nursery rime or the balladeer's "hey nonny no" and other meaningless refrains were once more seen as expressive and valuable for poetry. They have the same source as Rimbaud's prose poems or Laforgue's second line in his couplets—the unconscious, which Dujardin tried to capture. Breton's Surrealism was meant to make poets conscious of their unconscious.

Others than poets shared this pre-occupation, notably the medical psychologists. Janet, Charcot, and his pupils at the Salpêtrière Hospital were listening for clues to disease of the mind in the unpremeditated utterance of disturbed patients, while William James was analyzing and giving a technical description of the stream of consciousness, later so fruitful in the novel. The writers did not imitate or learn from the therapists, or vice versa, but it is worth noting the parallel, by which the poets were to become observers and

---

"We'll to the Woods No More." (The title comes from a child's song for round dancing: *Nous n'irons plus au bois, les lauriers sont coupés*—the laurels have been cut.)

recorders, like apprentices in science, the modern monster they said they despised.

That the obsession with language is not an interpretation imposed after the fact by the generalizing historian can be proved by quoting the poet who is perhaps the best representative of the eclecticism I have sketched. I mean Guillaume Apollinaire. I recall, to begin with, how he liked to amuse my childish mind, as I sat on his knee, by telling me that some grown-up word such as "tonsils" (*amygdales*) could mean "kitchen stove." Delighted, I would ask for another and another and then wonder when this magic change would come about: "When I make it happen." But the poet was in earnest, as I found out later when I read:

> O bouches l'homme est à la recherche d'un nouveau langage
> . . . .
> On veut de nouveaux sons de nouveaux sons de nouveaux sons
> . . . .
> Et que tout ait un nom nouveau.

To read modern French poetry—and other kinds as well—means therefore to recapture the hidden connections between the words, disparate on the surface, that spontaneous thought has juxtaposed in the inner soliloquy. The poet's image, the old *métaphore hardie*, is no longer a conscious extension of an idea; it is the product of watchfulness, the wait for kinship between non-thoughts or pre-thoughts.

For the poet, of course, the need for selection and organization remains, at least in poetry that is not automatic or aleatory; and it is here that the question of form, even of rules, returns. If the material of poetry is free of internal logic as well as of external representation, and verbal expression is free of grammar and semantics, what are the chances that a piece of writing that takes advantage of every latitude will arouse a reader's interest and evoke anything?

Granted, it is the pressure of modern life with its bombardment of simultaneous signals, its over-stimulation of the mind, that is being rendered in words and that justifies all the techniques of discordance. But the same mind is still unified while writing, even if the focus shifts with varying intentions. That unity is also needed if the poem

---

O mouths Man is in search of a new language. . . . / We want new sounds new sounds new sounds. . . . / And that everything should have a new name. ("La Victoire," *Calligrammes*)

is a mystery to be worked out: the reader's mind must be placated by a pattern of some kind. So at this point the impatience to be free often turns a somersault and declares that the role of poetry is to organize the disparate, not merely note it down. The passion for freedom breeds the rage for order.

Valéry's poetry is built on this conviction. The last of Mallarmé's disciples, Valéry is also the last to abide by the rules of Romanticist prosody. If he ever escaped into free verse, he never published the results. All his freedom is invested in imagery and harmony. He uses the alexandrine and some of the shorter forms, the traditional rime schemes and cesuras, makes gentle inversions and observes the rule against hiatus—all this with but slight and occasional licenses that only heighten the effect of poised regularity. As for diction and grammar, they yield to comprehension at once, without any of the imbrications of sense that Mallarmé found necessary to spur his laggard muse. The force of Valéry's images is in fact redoubled by their grammatical knitting together. In *Ebauche d'un serpent*, the original seducer snake addresses the sun with respectful lucidity:

> Verse-moi ta brute chaleur,
> Où vient ma paresse glacée
> Rêvasser de quelque malheur
> Selon ma nature enlacée . . .
> Ce lieu charmant qui vit la chair
> Choir et se joindre m'est très cher!
>
> Ma fureur, ici, se fait mûre:
> Je la conseille et la recuis,
> Je m'écoute, et dans mes circuits,
> Ma méditation murmure . . .

The snake nature appears in nearly every line thanks to the contraction of images: ice-cold laziness; twining nature; devious thought that ripens, talks to itself, and makes anger boil into fury,

---

"Sketch of a serpent" (The dots are suspensive, not signs of omission.) Pour on me your crude heat, / Where my ice-cold laziness / Comes to dream up some misfortune / In keeping with my twining nature . . . / This charming spot which saw Flesh / Fall and embrace is dear to me! / My fury here ripens; I give it counsel and reheat it / I pay heed to myself, and in my circlings / My meditation murmurs. (*Charmes*)

which is then ripe for the misfortune being planned. All of this makes dear the site where an earlier plot succeeded in causing Flesh to succumb and unite sexually. The harmony follows the sense at a steady pace—no jerky motion for this gliding conspirator. Glacée gives the keynote of the first quatrain, repeated in rêvasser and enlacée. Next chair, choir, and cher sound luscious and contrast with the previous iciness; after which the interplay of f's, hard c's, and m's makes good music, thanks to the meanings that accompany the sounds.

I suggested earlier that the modernity of Valéry and other poets lay in concentration of effect. Fifty years before Valéry, paresse glacée and nature enlacée would not have been possible so close together, not because poets were unable to think that way, but because their readers would have refused to do so. The public was gradually educated by a more and more rapid shorthand. Compare Valéry's unremitting contractions with Hugo's strong moves toward the same end. Hugo's vision of a lone figure on a cliff at dusk generated le pâtre promontoire (the shepherd headland) that proved infamous before it became famous. In another poem he has the noirs oiseaux du taillis héraldique (blackbirds of the heraldic thicket). The crowding of the symbols of heraldry on a knight's shield makes the thicket. He also speaks of elms in a storm showing "ragged, angered profiles"; and not infrequently his lines make leaps as striking as some of Rimbaud's. For instance, without explicit context, we come upon:

> Passez, souffles du ciel.
> Dieu seul connaît la nuit.

But in Hugo the poem is not an unbroken series of such raccourcis. The poet still consults the reader's convenience, communicates; he represents, instead of thrusting an object, that is, presenting it only, as does modern work. The difference corresponds to the shift in the poet's place. He is no longer prophetic and hortatory—at least on the surface. Nowadays, there is no public poetry—about events, issues, attitudes—only the private expression of private impressions. The audience has been trained to interpret this object and find the message within. Since the object is most often a rendering of some aspect of the contemporary world—the immediate, as Gide pointed

---

Sweep on, winds of heaven. / Only God knows the night. ("L'aigle du casque," Légende des Siècles)

out, because faith in the future is lacking—the message tends to be much the same on many occasions: the badness of life and of our life. Accordingly, one might have supposed that the desperate or cynical frame of mind woud have found utterance not alone in prose poems such as Rimbaud's, but also and more thunderingly in some large panorama of *vers libre* of the kind Whitman wrote—long *rythmes* without links between them, like the Psalms—an accumulation of free outbursts, but hostile instead of enthusiastic like Whitman's. Paul Fort did essay such an epic style in his *Ballades françaises*. Alas, like Whitman's *Leaves*, they are celebratory!

> Plus loin encor s'étage une contrée plus belle, où
> luisent des pommiers près de leur ombre ronde, Là,
> dans un creux huileux de calme, le soleil, où vit
> une prairie fait battre une émeraude.

It turns out, too, that within these leisurely descriptive paragraphs there are frequent stretches of meter and some inner rimes. One finds alexandrines and decasyllabics, but the count may be in doubt, because Paul Fort plays fast and loose with the mute *e*—now you hear it, now you don't. The "freedom" is intermittent and typographical, which is something, but not the Inferno I was looking for. Closer to it are a few poems by the Belgian Verhaeren in his *Villes tentaculaires*, which deal with the urban industrial landscape—notably London— and a few by another foreigner writing in French, Apollinaire. His give in long detailing lines the very opposite of "Beauty elevating the Soul":

> Tu es debout devant le zinc d'un bar crapuleux
> Tu prends un café à deux sous parmi les malheureux
> Tu es la nuit dans un grand restaurant
> Ces femmes ne sont pas méchantes elles ont des soucis cependant
> Toutes même la plus laide a fait souffrir son amant
>
> Elle est la fille d'un sergent de ville de Jersey
> Ses mains que je n'avais jamais vues sont dures et gercées
> J'ai une pitié immense pour les coutures de son ventre

Further still, a fairer region, where appletrees glow near their round shadows. There, in a calm hollow made shiny like oil, the sun, under which a meadow comes to life, sparks an emerald. ("Le Bercement du monde," *Ballades françaises*, 1ère série)

J'humilie maintenant à une pauvre fille au rire horrible ma bouche
Tu es seul le matin va venir

But even this form, with casual riming retained for a modicum of order, was a temporary choice. In other pieces, sad or gay, Apollinaire returns to the quasi traditional: riming quatrains, little songs in eight-syllable lines riming regularly, stanzas combining seven with two or ten with six, and toward the end of his brief life, the alexandrine in full dress:

> Si je mourais là-bas sur le front de l'armée
> Tu pleurerais un jour, O Lou, ma bien-aimée.

True, the rimes throughout are not punctilious, merely solid; the next lines pair *meurt* (in *t*) with *fleurs* (in *s*), but scruple about final consonants has long since been overcome. What is important is that meter, rhythm, cesura, hiatus are all back in their places as if nothing had happened since the *assouplissement* of the twelve-syllable line in the first half of the nineteenth century.

Is this a recovery of rights by Banville, the treatise-maker? Or by the language itself? Or are the poets weary of escapes that do not satisfy? No, freedom has not been abandoned, but redefined. *Vers libres* are still being written; so are prose poems; rime is not compulsory; assonance or approximate rime often replaces it; and violations of the strict rules, Neo-classic or Romanticist, cause no shudders—nor cheers. There is no one style for poets collectively; no poetics of the age; everything answers to the individual will, which is the definition of anarchy. And anarchy is an excellent thing when it can be had without grief or bloodshed.

Yet one more fact deserves notice: in the poetic free-for-all, the

---

You're standing up at the counter of a disreputable bar / You take a coffee for two cents among the wretches there / You are at night in a big restaurant / These women are not bad they have worries though / All even the ugliest has made her lover suffer / She is the daughter of a policeman in the island of Jersey / Her hands which I had never seen are hard and frostbitten / I feel an immense pity for the stitches in her belly / Now I humiliate my lips to a poor wench with a hideous laugh / You are alone morning is about to come. ("Zone," *Alcools*)

If I should die out there, at the front with the army / You would weep for a day, O Lou, my beloved.

alexandrine and other French meters are still being used, and more often than free lines. This is not an impression; someone has counted.° The measured rhythm need not govern an entire piece; it crops up unexpectedly; perhaps the poet found it leaping at him like a flying fish. At any rate, one thoughtful critic has concluded that "When all is said, the mould which gives the most freedom, which affords without strain the greatest variety in the disposition of measures, may well be the sequence of alexandrines."° Others disagree and discuss "the old age" or "the fate" of *Alexandre*, generally engulfing in his demise all other current forms.° *Vers libre* is seen as done with too, because its mission was to kill syllabic meter, and with it dead, the point of the mayhem disappears. Modern poetry would then be altogether at an end. But in the arts public burial is not always definitive. There is always a chance that the corpse will revive as a young man.

"Let every land have joy of its poet," said Gissing, "for the poet is the land itself." Even truer, the poet is the language itself. The land changes contour and extent with political vicissitudes, but the language, despite all *its* changes, retains a fixed character. The French vowels *si nuancées*, as Valéry remarked, and so eager for elision; the consonants ever subject to purposeful attrition; the volatile accentuation; the natural supply of rimes; the instrumental range of the mute *e;* the fluidity born of analytic expression, which excludes compound adjectives ahead of nouns and agglutinative phrasing anywhere—all this has formed but one poetic medium for French poets over seven centuries. *The Song of Roland,* to be sure, has an alien sound, no longer Latin, not yet French. But come the thirteenth century, and the French poet's voice is heard in accents we recognize even when we have not learned all the words. The poet's avatars show different tempers and powers, shifting fads of diction and speech; but throughout, his is the voice of the language grown conscious of itself: "I am a poet. Let us see what can be done with this given shapeless mass of words." He sings, and regardless of who repeats his song, we catch its harmony. We hear one voice, modulating, in Jean de Meung, Villon, Ronsard, Corneille, Racine, Molière, Hugo, Musset, Baudelaire, Rimbaud, Valéry, Eluard, and those who came between—and shall hear it again in those who are to come after.

Victor Hugo

LES DJINNS

(Les Orientales)

LES DJINNS

E como i gru van cantando lor lai
Facendo in aer di se lunga riga,
Cosi vid' io venir traendo guai
Ombre portate dalla detta briga.
—Dante

MURS, ville,
Et port,
Asile
De mort,
Mer grise
Où brise
La brise,
Tout dort.

Dans la plaine
Naît un bruit.
C'est l'haleine
De la nuit.
Elle brame
Comme une âme
Qu'une flamme
Toujours suit!

La voix plus haute
Semble un grelot.
D'un nain qui saute
C'est le galop.
Il fuit, s'élance,
Puis en cadence
Sur un pied danse
Au bout d'un flot.

EVIL SPIRITS

And like the cranes which, screaming plaints forlorn,
Make long lines in the air through which they fly,
Thus I saw shades upon that tempest borne
Who groaned and wailed as they were carried by.
                                        —Dante

Town, walls,
And port,
Death-halls
And court,
Gray seas
Where sweeps
The breeze—
All sleeps.

From the plain
Comes a sound:
'Tis the night's
Breath of pain,
'Tis the dole
Of a soul
Phantom lights
Ruthless hound.

The louder stave
Is like a chime.
Along it trips
A dwarf, who hops
Who gallops, skips,
And keeping time,
On one foot bobs
Atop a wave.

La rumeur approche,
L'écho la redit.
C'est comme la cloche
D'un couvent maudit;
Comme un bruit de foule,
Qui tonne et qui roule,
Et tantôt s'écroule,
Et tantôt grandit.

Dieu! la voix sépulcrale
Des Djinns! . . . Quel bruit ils font!
Fuyons sous la spirale
De l'escalier profond.
Déjà s'éteint ma lampe,
Et l'ombre de la rampe,
Qui le long du mur rampe,
Monte jusqu'au plafond.

C'est l'essaim des Djinns qui passe,
Et tourbillonne en sifflant!
Les ifs, que leur vol fracasse,
Craquent comme un pin brûlant.
Leur troupeau, lourd et rapide,
Volant dans l'espace vide,
Semble un nuage livide
Qui porte un éclair au flanc.

Ils sont tout près!—Tenons fermée
Cette salle, où nous les narguons.
Quel bruit dehors! Hideuse armée
De vampires et de dragons!
La poutre du toit descellée
Ploie ainsi qu'une herbe mouillée,
Et la vieille porte rouillée
Tremble, à déraciner ses gonds!

Clamors growing loud
Echo like a dirge
Or the fatal spell
Of a cursed knell—
Murmurs of a crowd,
Thunders that unroll,
Now a dying toll,
Now a welling surge.

God! The sepulcral-voiced!
The Djinns! They rend the air!
Quick! Under the retreat—
The spiral of the stair.
Already blinks the lamp
And the shadows that ramp
Where wall and staircase meet
Climb to the topmost joist.

The swarm of Djinns is passing!
Their hissing whirlwind races,
The yews that their flight shatters
Crackle like a burning plank;
Their swift herd, heavy-massing,
Flies through the empty spaces,
A livid cloud that scatters
The lightning in its flank.

They are upon us! Shut in tight
This room where we may yet defy
Their fury. Hear them rage without!
Dragons, vampires, beings accurst!
The ceiling beam is loosed: though stout,
It bends—a twig beneath their might.
The old door shakes as if to try
In fear its rusty hinge to burst.

Cris de l'enfer! voix qui hurle et qui pleure!
L'horrible essaim, poussé par l'aquilon,
Sans doute, ô ciel! s'abat sur ma demeure.
Le mur fléchit sous le noir bataillon.
La maison crie et chancelle penchée,
Et l'on dirait que, du sol arrachée,
Ainsi qu'il chasse une feuille séchée,
Le vent la roule avec leur tourbillon!

Prophète! si ta main me sauve
De ces impurs démons des soirs,
J'irai prosterner mon front chauve
Devant tes sacrés encensoirs!
Fais que sur ces portes fidèles
Meure leur souffle d'étincelles,
Et qu'en vain l'ongle de leurs ailes
Grince et crie à ces vitraux noirs!

Ils sont passés!—Leur cohorte
S'envole, et fuit, et leurs pieds
Cessent de battre ma porte
De leurs coups multipliés.
L'air est plein d'un bruit de chaînes,
Et dans les forêts prochaines
Frissonnent tous les grands chênes,
Sous leur vol de feu pliés!

De leurs ailes lointaines
Le battement décroît,
Si confus dans les plaines,
Si faible, que l'on croit
Ouïr la sauterelle
Crier d'une voix grêle,
Ou pétiller la grêle
Sur le plomb d'un vieux toit.

Infernal shouts! Voices that howl and wail!
The frightful swarm, blown forth by Boreas,
Now stomps, O heavens, on my frail abode;
The walls give as the black battalions pass;
The structure screams and totters to its core.
It seems as if, uprooted from the sod,
And like a dry leaf that it drives before,
The wind would sweep it headlong in the gale.

Prophet! If thy hand but save me
From these foul demons of the night,
I will bow my head and lave me
And fulfill thy holy rite.
On these ever-faithful portals
Make their breath to burn in vain,
And let the claws of these immortals
Vainly scratch this darkened pane.

They are gone. The fiery troop
Soars aloft and flees; their feet,
Which innumerable roared,
On my door have ceased to beat.
Now on nearby woods they swoop
With a noise of clanking chains,
And the giant oak complains
As it bends beneath the horde.

From the flapping of wings
Growing less, one receives
Of their waning a proof,
Now so faint one believes
'Tis a cricket who sings
In a voice high and frail,
Or the patter of hail
On a lead-covered roof.

D'étranges syllabes
Nous viennent encor;
Ainsi, des arabes
Quand sonne le cor,
Un chant sur la grève
Par instants s'élève,
Et l'enfant qui rêve
Fait des rêves d'or.

Les Djinns funèbres,
Fils du trépas,
Dans les ténèbres
Pressent leurs pas;
Leur essaim gronde:
Ainsi, profonde,
Murmure une onde
Qu'on ne voit pas.

Ce bruit vague
Qui s'endort,
C'est la vague
Sur le bord;
C'est la plainte,
Presque éteinte,
D'une sainte
Pour un mort.

On doute
La nuit . . .
J'écoute:—
Tout fuit,
Tout passe;
L'espace
Efface
Le bruit.

Syllables forlorn
Still toward us creep—
Arab riders' call
Answering the horn . . .
Thus again they seem
Singing's rise and fall,
While the child asleep
Dreams a golden dream.

The dismal Djinns,
Dread sons of Doom,
Into the gloom
Press on their steps.
Their clamor thins;
So murmuring,
Flows in the depths
A hidden spring.

Vague sounds more—
Slumbering, or
Like the wave
Washed ashore,
Or the plaint
Soft and faint
Of a saint
On a grave.

At night
Disquiet . . .
But dread
Has fled—
No trace,
For space
Has drowned
All sound.

I made this approximation while an undergraduate and published
it two years later (under a pseudonym I use from time to time) in *The
Morningside*, vol. XVII, No. 2, February 1929. In reprinting it here I
have changed a dozen words or so, to get closer (possibly) to the
original.

REFERENCE NOTES

Page 2 Mannerism   Edmund Gosse, *From Shakespeare to Pope*, New York, 1885, was the first study to describe in detail the transition from Renaissance to Neo-classical in poetry and bring out the contributions of Waller and Denham.

3 should have been   André Gide, *Anthologie de la Poésie Française*, Paris, 1949, vii–viii.

5 one of eleven   Quoted in Emile Legouis, *Défense de la Poésie Française*, New York, 1912, 79.

6 service of poetry   Thomas De Quincey, "A Peripatetic Philosopher," *The Notebook of an English Opium Eater*, Boston, 1871, 242. (In some collections the essay is entitled "Walking Stewart.")

— whole French language   Walter Savage Landor, "The Abbé Delille and Walter Landor," *Imaginary Conversations*, Third Series, Boston, 1877, *passim*, but see especially pp. 3, 92ff., 100, 117, 123, 291, 295.

— many rocks for them   Matthew Arnold, "Heinrich Heine," *Essays in Criticism*, Third edition, 1875, 209.

— reminding us of one   Landor, *op. cit.* (see note to p. 6), 116.

7 in their language   Undated ms. printed in Kathleen Coburn, ed., *Inquiring Spirit: Coleridge*, Toronto, 1979, 156.

— in none supreme   Arnold, *Poems*, "To a Republican Friend, 1848," II.

9 care of themselves   Bishop Whately, *Elements of Rhetoric*, ed. D. Ehninger and D. Potter, Carbondale, 1963, 358*n*.

— *très nuancées*   Paul Valéry, quoted in Paul Robert, *Dictionnaire alphabétique et analogique de la langue française*, Paris 1973, p. 1928.

— *Maintenong*   Ronald Knox, *Still Dead*. London, 1934, 238.

10 steel say lum   H.G. Wells, *Tono Bungay*, Bk III, ch. 2.

— inside the book   L.D. Van Rooten, *Mots d'heures gousses rames*, New York, 1967.

12 length and forcefulness   Jeanne Varney Pleasants, *Etudes sur l'E muet*, Paris, 1956.

17 interest and importance   H.S. Bennett, *Chaucer and the Fifteenth Century*, New York, 1947, 8.

18 the historian Pasquier   *Recherches de la France* (1560), VII, ch. 7, 616.

— the same attempt   Jacques de la Taille, *La Manière de faire des vers en français comme en grec et en latin*, ed. Pierre Han, Chapel Hill, 1970.

19 if the line is to scan   Adolf Tobler, *Vom französischen Versbau*

alter und neuer Zeit, trans. from the 2nd ed. by Karl Breyl and Léopold Sudre (1885), repr. Geneva, 1972, 48.

21   never met before   Le Père Bouhours, "La langue française," *Entretiens d'Ariste et d'Eugène* (1671), ed. René Radouant, Paris, 1920, 55.

22   color and strangeness   Thomas Gray, "The language of Poetry," *Essays and Criticism*, ed. C.S. Northup, Boston, 1911, 133.

25   intellectual power   Théodore de Banville, *Petit traité de poésie française*, Paris, 1872, 53–54, 72–75.

27   all the Italian   Landor, *op. cit.* (see note to p. 6), Fifth Series: "The Emperor of China and Tsing-ti," 451.

—   sounded é, not è   Tobler, *op. cit.* (see note to p. 19), 155*n*. and Maurice Grammont, *Le Vers français*, Paris 1964, 348–349.

28   the rime exact   Paul Reboux and Charles Muller, *A la Manière de . . .* , Paris, 1926, 201.

—   to rime with it   George Perkins Marsh, *Lectures on the English Language*, New York, 1860, 501.

32   rather a barbarism   Abbé D'Olivet, "Observations sur Racine," *Remarques sur la langue française*, Paris, 1767, 13.

—   a diamond edge   Robert Lowell, "On Translating *Phèdre*," in *Phaedra and Figaro*, by Robert Lowell and Jacques Barzun, New York, 1960, 8.

34   character of the speaker   Richard Strauss and Romain Rolland, *Correspondence* (originally in *Cahiers Romain Rolland*, No. 3, Paris, 1951), trans. and ed. Rollo Myers, Berkeley, 1968, 37–38.

35   imagination and passion   See Odette de Mourgues, *An Anthology of French 17th-Century Lyric Poetry*, Oxford, 1966.

38   vivacity and exactitude   Marianne Moore, *The Fables of La Fontaine*, New York, 1954. The volume is a selection only, as is the far more accomplished version by Norman R. Shapiro, *Fifty Fables of La Fontaine*, Middletown, 1988.

40   no longer be sung   Voltaire, *Le Siècle de Louis XIV*, Appendice: Catalogue des Ecrivains, under "Quinault."

42   and raison d'être   The excellent essays edited by W.K. Wimsatt, *Versification: Major Language Types*, New York, 1972, are too summary to provide the required initiation.

—   of English literature   Legouis, *op. cit.*, see note to p. 5.

—   perceptive survey   Henry Francis Cary, *The Early French Poets*, ed. T. Earle Welby, London, 1923. This Campion Reprint No. II of the 1846 edition omits the translated examples from the poets discussed.

43   found in the Notes   The three books are: Clive Scott, *French Verse Art*, Cambridge, 1980; P. Mansell Jones, *The Background of Modern French Poetry*, Cambridge, 1968; and Peter Broome and Graham Chesters, *The Appreciation of Modern French Poetry: 1850–1950*, Cambridge, 1976.

— with the English   George P. Marsh, *Lectures on the English Language*, New York, 1860.

44 their right names   François de Salignac de la Mothe Fénelon, *Dialogues sur l'éloquence*, Paris, 1718, 159–60.

— and passionate   Fénelon, *Lettre à l'Académie*, ed. L. Beck, Paris, 1935, 23.

— he really wants   *Ibid.*, 52–55, 80-81.

— as well as comedy   *Ibid.*, 78, 88.

45 ours simply *justes*   Antoine Rivarol, *De l'Universalité de la langue française*, ed. W.W. Comfort, New York, 1919, 45.

— *forçant son naturel*   *Ibid.*, 46.

— very good reading   The *Poem on the Lisbon Disaster* has been translated into English under that title by Anthony Hecht, Lincoln, Mass., 1977.

52 character of the emotion   Albert Cassagne, *Versification et métrique de Baudelaire*, Paris, 1906, 64.

53 French verse   Grammont, *op. cit.* (see note to p. 27), 381.

57 *porteu, chasseu*   François Génin, *Des Variations du langage francais depuis le XIIè siecle*, Paris, 1845, 50–52, 68–69.

59 to achieve harmony   An excellent guide to scanning and pronouncing French verse is available: Roy Lewis, *On Reading French Verse*, Oxford, 1982.

61 Distinction of Merit   William Blake, Annotations to Sir Joshua Reynolds' *Discourses* (1808), Geoffrey Keynes, ed., *Poetry and Prose of William Blake*, New York, 1927, 977.

— T'[*u*]en as menti   Gérard de Nerval, "Chansons et légendes du Valois," *Les Filles du feu, Oeuvres*, ed. Jean Richer, Paris, 1974, 274–281.

67 of the whole century   J.-P. Sartre in *L'Idiot de la famille*, quoted by Victor Brombert in *Victor Hugo and the Visionary Novel*, Cambridge (Mass.), 1984, 3.

69 a Pythian ode   A[lgernon] C[harles] S[winburne], "Victor Hugo," in *Encyclopedia Britannica*, 11th edition (1910), v. 13, 864.

71 to slight Hugo   Henri Peyre, *Victor Hugo: Philosophy and Poetry* (1972), trans. Roda P. Roberts, University (Alabama), 1980, 14.

72 what is meant   The line is from *The Tempest*, I, 2, 408.

75 half-witted sheep   J.K. Stephen, "Wordsworth: a Sonnet," in *The New Oxford Book of Light Verse*, ed. Kingsley Amis, Oxford, 1978, 176.

— and the alliteration   Justin O'Brien, "Hugo,—hélas!", *The French Review*, v. 37, no. 5, April 1964, 554–556.

— *de la poésie moderne*   *Ibid.*, 556.

76 and spread forth   André Gide, *The Journals of*, trans. Justin O'Brien, New York, 1949, III, 80.

— it sounds with   Victor Hugo, "Tas de pierres," *Postscriptum de ma vie*, Paris, 1901, III, 55.

76   as in Hamlet's   George Moore, *Confessions of a Young Man* (1888), ed. Floyd Dell, New York, 1917, 196–197. The soliloquy Moore refers to is that of Don Carlos (Charles V) in Hugo's *Hernani*, IV, 2.

77   for lyric use   The poem and the essay are in *Swinburne: New Writings*, ed. Cecil Y. Lang, Syracuse, N.Y., 1964, 7–10, 57.

78   know about verse   Banville, *op. cit.* (see note to p. 25), 76.

— for their *hardiesses*   Sainte-Beuve set forth their claims in 1828 in his *Tableau historique et critique de la poésie française et du théâtre français du XVIè siècle*.

87   cannot *feel* there   Gide, *Anthologie, op. cit.* (see note to p. 3), xlii.

— the mode of expression   Gérard de Nerval, *Oeuvres, op. cit.* (see note to p. 61), 1266.

88   And ride mankind   Ralph Waldo Emerson, "Ode inscribed to W.H. Channing."

89   no affectation but fact   Roger L. Williams, *The Horror of Life*, Chicago, 1980.

91   the more beautiful   Baudelaire, *Les Fleurs du Mal*, XXIV.

94   it is all one   Baudelaire, "Les Foules," *Petits Poèmes en Prose*, XII.

— of that, Proudhon?   Ibid., "Assommons les pauvres," XLIX. The challenge to Proudhon is in the ms., not the printed version. There is evidence that the piece is not ironic.

— upheavals of conscience   Ibid., Preface-dedication to Arsène Houssaye.

— toward the Earth   Ibid., "Enivrez-vous," XXXII.

95   of self-consciousness   John Simon, *The Prose Poem as a Genre in 19th-Century European Literature*, New York, 1987. See also: *The Prose Poem in France*, ed. Mary Ann Caws and Hermine Riffaterre, New York, 1983.

96   every scheme and idea   See Valéry, "Situation de Baudelaire," *Variété II*, Paris, 1930, 145ff.

97   and nothing more   George Brimley, "Tennyson's Poems," *Essays* (1858), New York, 1861, 39.

98   Unanimism   A.J. George, *Lamartine and Romantic Unanimism*, New York, 1940. A definition of Unanimism by the inventor of the name, Jules Romains, is given by him in his *Problèmes d'aujourd'hui*, Paris, 1931, 157.

101   bridle of rime   Banville, *op. cit.*, (see note to p. 25), 95–96.

102   and theorizing   See Robert Gibson, *Modern French Poets on Poetry*, Cambridge, 1961.

— moment decides   Rémy de Gourmont, "Dissociation," *La Culture des idées*, quoted by Charles Chassé in *Les Clés de Mallarmé*, Paris, 1954, 9. (The cover of Chassé's book, unlike the title page, spells the key word *Clefs*.) Gourmont's essay is translated in *Selected Writings*, ed. and trans. Glenn S. Bourne, Ann Arbor, 1966.

103   on sounds, not on sense   Gourmont, *Le livre des masques*, quoted by Hugo P. Thieme, *Essai sur l'histoire du vers français* (1916), New York, 1971, 87.

— among the etymologies   Chassé, *op. cit.* (see note to p. 102), 99–209.

107   resolve the doubts   Romain Rolland, *Musiciens d'aujourd'hui*, Paris, 1908, 7.

108   fourth syllable   Jean Mazaleyrat quoted in Clive Scott, *op. cit.* (see note to p. 43), 51.

— pitiable young man   Arthur Rimbaud, "Les Déserts de l'amour, Avertissement," in *Oeuvres*, ed. Paul Claudel, Paris, 1924, 101.

109   and trusted him   *Ibid.*, Preface by Claudel, 9, 17.

110   is still around   "Qu'est ce pour nous, mon coeur."

— vicious personalities   Laurent Tailhade, *Au Pays du Mufle*, Paris, 1891, 19, 71ff.

111   for expressiveness   F.T. Marinetti, *Les Mots en liberté futuristes*, Milan, 1919, 14, 19, 24–25, 51.

— not a dope   André Breton, *Manifeste du Surréalisme*, Paris, 1924, 43, 52–53.

112   psychological reality   A detailed analysis of the innovations is in A.G. Cameron, *E. and J. de Goncourt: Selections*, New York, 1898, Appendix II, 326–346.

113   *vers libres* on record   The earlier meanings of the term are mentioned on pp. 36, 37, 44, 67, 99, and 13ff. But what is now *vers libre* was theorized about as early as the sixteenth century.

114   any such influence   P. Mansell Jones, *op. cit.* (see note to p. 43), 159ff.

— opposite of the truth   Amy Lowell, *Six French Poets*, New York, 1916, 116. For nine more poets of the period, see Ezra Pound, *Instigations*, New York, 1920, Part I. See also: Georges-Emmanuel Chancier, *La Poésie et ses environs*, Paris, 1973.

115   called leonine   Littré says that the origin of the name is in doubt. Such verses contained repetitions of the same sound, particularly in the riming words.

— *vous ressemblera*   Tristan Tzara, *Seven Dada Manifestos and Lampisteries*, trans. Barbara Wright, New York, 1981, 39. See also: "L'apport de Tzara" in Micheline Tison-Braun, *Dada et le Surréalisme*, Paris, 1965, 64–65.

118   several words   Charles Péguy, "Victor-Marie, Comte Hugo," *Oeuvres Complètes*, ed. André Suarès, Paris, 1916, IV, 432.

— a deeper order   *Ibid.*, 433.

119 a coherent unit   "A Poet's Theories," [Entries from Eluard's diary], ed. David Wise, *Granta* (Cambridge), March 10, 1962, 29–30.

120 a syntactical minimum   Edouard Dujardin, *We'll to the Woods No More*, trans. Stuart Gilbert, New York, 1938, 154. This English text is still in print; the French is not. I have slightly modified the translated passage to come closer to the original.

126 someone has counted   Frédéric Deloffre, *Le vers français*, 2nd ed. Paris, 1973, 165–166.

— of alexandrines   Robert Champigny, *Le Genre poétique*, Monte Carlo, 1963, 61. Quoted in Clive Scott, *op. cit.* (see note to p. 43), 18.

— other current forms   The most analytic is Jacques Roubaud, *La vieillesse d'Alexandre, essai sur quelques états récents du vers français*, Paris, 1978.

ACKNOWLEDGMENTS

I am deeply indebted, and grateful, to my three learned friends John Hollander, James Laughlin, and Katherine Reeve for reading my text in typescript. Their devoted attention saved me from errors stupid and clever, as well as helped me to greater lucidity. Thanks to their generous aid, I am encouraged to believe that this essay may serve the purpose I had in writing it, which was to entice readers into the precincts of its great subject.